Daniel L. Langford, MSW, DMin

The Pastor's Family
The Challenges of Family Life and Pastoral Responsibilities

Pre-publication
REVIEWS,
COMMENTARIES,
EVALUATIONS . . .

"**D**an Langford invites us to share his struggle to keep in balance his life as father, husband, and pastor. Introspective, insightful, and probing in its honesty, this book lays bare the human matrix of the pastor's family as a therapeutic guide to healing and empowering the spiritual ministry of the pastor's calling.

Pastors, would-be pastors, and church members should read this compelling book for its diagnostic value as well as for its inspired vision. The health and well-being of the pastor's family is the spiritual core of the church's life and ministry."

Ray S. Anderson, PhD
Professor of Theology and Ministry,
Fuller Theological Seminary, Pasadena, CA

More pre-publication
REVIEWS, COMMENTARIES, EVALUATIONS . . .

"*The Pastor's Family* is a rich text expressed with well-founded reason, clarity, and passion. Dr. Langford undertook an extraordinary odyssey toward his and his family's attainment of their human authenticity. His suffering in the knowledge of neglecting his family lead him to recognize and respect his wife's and children's dignity, individuality, and unique life goals. He discovered what it means to be equal and what it means to be free. Through his book and changed behavior, he was redeemed.

This book—a true psychosociocultural exploration of the three interacting processes producing behavior, an honest assessment of himself and his family's development as they confronted and survived crucial social situations, a struggle yielding life's wisdom—should be required reading not only for ministers of all faiths but also for educators, human services practitioners, and all health care providers. In fact, any man or woman feeling unfulfilled, dissatisfied, or empty with work, career, family, or life will be inspired by the author's example to undertake the great task of creating powerful foundations for living fully. Dr. Langford and his family's self-awareness quest led them to what is ultimately central and of utmost value in life: to love fully and care for family."

Juan D. Hernández
Director,
Division of Social Work,
California State University,
Sacramento

"There is no doubt in my mind that one's family pays a price for being in ministry. Langford's book, however, provides hope that with proper attention to one's family it is possible to prevent a lot of damage. The book is personal, poignant, and perceptive. It unmasks the real perils of ministry and points to preventative strategies. It is, above all, a book of hope for clergy couples. There is a lot we can all learn from the mistakes others have made in ministry, and this book is an ideal resource for such learning."

Archibald D. Hart, PhD
Professor of Psychology,
Graduate School of Psychology,
Fuller Theological Seminary,
Pasadena, CA

The Haworth Pastoral Press
An Imprint of The Haworth Press, Inc.

The Pastor's Family
The Challenges of Family Life and Pastoral Responsibilities

THE HAWORTH PASTORAL PRESS
Religion and Mental Health
Harold G. Koenig, MD
Senior Editor

New, Recent, and Forthcoming Titles:

A Gospel for the Mature Years: Finding Fulfillment by Knowing and Using Your Gifts by Harold Koenig, Tracy Lamar, and Betty Lamar

Is Religion Good for Your Health? The Effects of Religion on Physical and Mental Health by Harold Koenig

Adventures in Senior Living: Learning How to Make Retirement Meaningful and Enjoyable by J. Lawrence Driskill

Dying, Grieving, Faith, and Family: A Pastoral Care Approach by George W. Bowman

The Pastoral Care of Depression: A Guidebook by Binford W. Gilbert

Understanding Clergy Misconduct in Religious Systems: Scapegoating, Family Secrets, and the Abuse of Power by Candace R. Benyei

What the Dying Teach Us: Lessons on Living by Samuel Lee Oliver

The Pastor's Family: The Challenges of Family Life and Pastoral Responsibilities by Daniel L. Langford

Grief Education for Caregivers of the Elderly by Junietta Baker McCall

Somebody's Knocking at Your Door: AIDS and the African-American Church by Ronald Jeffrey Weatherford and Carole Boston Weatherford

The Pastor's Family
The Challenges of Family Life and Pastoral Responsibilities

Daniel L. Langford, MSW, DMin

The Haworth Pastoral Press
An Imprint of The Haworth Press, Inc.
New York • London

Published by

The Haworth Pastoral Press, an imprint of The Haworth Press, Inc., 10 Alice Street, Binghamton, NY 13904-1580

Cover design by Monica L. Seifert.

Library of Congress Cataloging-in-Publication Data

Langford, Daniel L.
The pastor's family: the challenges of family life and pastoral responsibilities / Daniel L. Langford.
    p. cm.
Includes bibliographical references and index.
ISBN 0-7890-0585-9 (alk. paper).
1. Clergy—Family relationships. 2. Clergy—Office. I. Title.
BV4396.L36 1998
253'.22—dc21
                                      98-18461
                                          CIP

To Diana, Daniel Aaron, and Deanna,
the heroes of The Pastor's Family

ABOUT THE AUTHOR

Daniel L. Langford, MSW, DMin, has been a nursing home social worker, public school teacher, and pastor/church planter in California. He is a member of the National Association of Social Workers and is committed to improving the lives of oppressed individuals and communities in contemporary society.

CONTENTS

SECTION III: THE PASTOR AND HIS FAMILY

SECTION IV: THE PASTOR AND PERSONAL RECOVERY

Foreword

Pastoral expectations come from many sources. What pastors expect of themselves is a major source. Another is what various groups and individuals within the local church expect when extending a call, yet do not always share with the candidate. Others are what the Lord of the Church expects; what the spouse and pastoral family expect; and what colleagues in ministry expect. Then, add to this mix those of the denomination and community at large. What an impossible profile to figure out, especially when few of those involved are really listening to the Lord of the Church who alone knows how things need to be.

Dr. Langford's insightful and intimate sharing in this book captures what many clergy families are heir to and too often fail to admit. He and Diana, while unique in their journey, reflect their commonality with other sojourners. This book needs to be read by pastors, spouses, and children, lay leaders of all denominations, and seminary professors. It is in studying their journey that God's Spirit may illuminate our own with fuller clarity and understanding. We all suffer from "expectation giganteous." It can be fatal to marriages, families, and ministries when left untreated.

When God's priorities are allowed to prevail, the local church pastor has four of them to juggle on a daily basis.

First, the *personal:* being God's person and a seeker of His face. Being a person after God's own heart. Keeping this as one's major priority in all ways at all times. Without this, ministry becomes common and often lacking "heartfulness." To be God's person is to be heartful.

Second, the *marital:* being God's person in the life of one's partner. Knowing this primary relationship is key to all other human relating, it tells us best what is inside us. We live life from the inside out. This is at the heart of the relational circle as it moves outward to all others.

Third, the *familial:* being God's person in the life of one's family and extended family. Each PK (preacher's kid) has more than enough pressure and stress without more coming from within the family itself. The family is to be his or her safe place. Here honest expectations need to be defined and refined.

Fourth, the *pastoral:* being God's person in the life of one's congregation, community, denomination or fellowship, and world. Being a leader and resource person to people under similar priorities. We are co-sojourners in faith, living out God's priorities.

However, few see it this way, including many new pastors. There's the rub. To reorder these priorities in any other way is to violate His call. The call to ministry is always within the context of God's calling to being, then to doing. Righteousness is more than being right; it is right relating. Ministry is always within the context of right relating. We may be forgiven some bad sermons but never bad relationships.

Because of Dan's broad educational background, training, life experiences, and maturity, along with his personal commitment to God, Diana, their kids, and ministry, he has come to recognize and realize his earlier misperceptions of the pastoral calling. Through the Spirit's prompting and Diana's encouragement, perceptions began to change. God's side of one's calling may be quite clear but the personal side may be shrouded in mystery, misunderstanding, fantasy, and denial. It demands honest self-understanding and examination.

Some of the pastor's real needs may be met through ministry; however, that is not its objective nor is it to be one's focus. Being called to serve means giving of one's self in dependable ways for the meeting of real needs of others, to the glory of God. When one is in it for one's own unfulfilled needs, then all suffer—God, the person, partner, family, church, and Kingdom.

Ministry is not a nine-to-five job with two days off a week, and without overtime. No profession is. In calling one to the ministry, God has a task to be fulfilled. He also empowers the one called so it can be fulfilled meaningfully. But each one called brings personal baggage, unmet needs, relational skills or their lack, spiritual gifts, and a heart filled with definite expectations. Finding the best focus, managing a schedule, fielding the urgent, establishing and maintaining healthy relationships and boundaries, and above all, being God's person, impact how ministry will be practiced and a local church served. Once the reader has wrestled with Dan's basic questions, then one can move on into all these other areas of consideration.

I have been an observer of Dan and Diana's transitioning in recent years, and I praise their relationship. I hope God uses them in mentoring many of our colleagues in ministry. I wish I had known others like them—and read such a book—when I left seminary in the 1960s to conquer the world. It would have been a very different journey.

Having served a major denomination as a Pastor to Pastors and serving as a specialist in conflict resolution, I am deeply committed to all those serving God on the front lines of ministerial practice. They are some of faith's heroes. But too many end up casualties of their own expectations and those of others. How different things would be if persons called to the ministry understood themselves better and God's priorities truly prevailed. How different things would be if pastors and families and local churches and seminaries had an advocate who understood these priorities and taught them to all concerned.

Most pastors, lay leaders, and members perceive their local church as "their church." Their actions betray this faulty theology. It is supposed to be His, glorifying Him. He calls us into partnership with Himself but He is to be in control. His expectations are what count. Things will be different when He again regains control. What a wonderful day that will be!

Emil J. Authelet Jr., DMin
Consultant in Church Renewal
and Conflict Resolution
Vallejo, California

Preface

I first began writing *The Pastor's Family* in the fall of 1989. The story dates back to my family's first year in ministry, which was 1983. I thought we had already been through plenty of changes then. Nevertheless, the nine years that I took to prepare this story have punctuated the reality that life indeed goes on; we constantly undergo change.

Since I began to write this story, I have watched my son make the transition from adolescence to adulthood. Daniel Aaron is now the father of his own son, and he has only just begun the journey of life with his new family. Likewise, my daughter entered the sixth grade in 1989. She is now in the Air Force and a graduate of College of the Redwoods, Eureka, California.

Many other passages occurred during this period. My father died in 1990. My wife and I lost a business; we went through a period of homelessness; we lost and gained employment. We moved four times in the past nine years.

Life goes on, and changes occur at every moment. Accordingly, I am standing midstream in a story that will look far different in the years to come. Nevertheless, here is my family's tale at this moment in time.

* * *

I am a male pastor, and I realize I have neglected my family because I failed to prioritize time with them and for them in my life as a minister. *The Pastor's Family* is the story of how I was compelled to face this neglect and do something about it.

My wife and children candidly share their feelings and experiences, and we have attempted, through our struggles, to find a more acceptable model of ministry that gives priority and respect to the male pastor's family.

I have not yet done research on how families headed by a female pastor are doing. Nevertheless, I would postulate that female pastors treat their families better than male pastors do. The reason I believe this to be true is related to the dark side of Western culture. Because of the way our society is structured, a considerable number of women have experienced the neglect and oppression of males. In addition, some research that examines the role of women in our society suggests that women do not abandon relationships for careers. Joan Berzoff offers this convincing argument:

> The new psychology of women has come to see women as psychologically defined through their relationships. Women's experiences of connectedness—mothering and nurturing and caretaking—have come to be valued as female occupations that catalyze the development of others and as strengths that catalyze self-development.[1]

Whereas times are changing and more women are focusing on careers over families, the dilemma of family abandonment for a career still appears to be a unique male problem. To redefine the problem, females predominantly find identity in relationships, while males predominantly find identity in a profession—hence, the neglect of the family. Correspondingly, neglect of the pastor's family will continue to be a unique problem of male pastors.

Why this occurs remains a mystery. I don't understand whether male choices are dictated by culture or whether they are a part of innate, male human nature. Nevertheless, *The Pastor's Family* tells my story and presents my conviction that family neglect for the sake of career is wrong. I contend that the male worldview and the "good old boy" attitudes of Christian culture that have condoned by default the neglect of the pastor's family need to be overhauled.

I heed Paul's command: "Husbands love your wives just as Christ loved the church . . ." (Ephesians 5:25, NIV). Accordingly, I will tell you of my failures to care for my family, but also, I will tell you how I am trying to learn what it means to love and to give myself away to my wife, my children, my family—*The Pastor's Family.*

Daniel L. Langford

SECTION I:
THE PASTOR AND HIS SPOUSE

Chapter 1

"Where Is Dad?"
"Where Is My Husband?"

PASTOR ABANDONS FAMILY
FOR THE MINISTRY

This would be the headline if my story were front-page news. At first, I did not understand what I had done, but the accusation is true. I deserted my family, and I am not alone. Preachers' kids and pastors' wives from innumerable churches and denominations have experienced a culturally accepted wholesale neglect that has been woven into a deficient model of ministry. The most common perpetrators of this neglect are male pastors.

Taking responsibility for this abandonment causes intense emotional pain. I love my family, and I uphold family values in the pulpit. I have preached, "Care for your loved ones! Heed the biblical warning that family neglect is worse than unbelief!" My preaching has been fervent. Yet despite this eloquence, my wife and children could have marched with placards shouting, "Hey preacher! Practice what you preach!"

My family suffered emotional neglect and physical desertion that originated in a failure to balance the demands of ministry with the needs of the family. I recognize there is no instant solution to resolve these imbalances; the correction is going to take time. Each day will require a fresh look. With every dawn, I am challenged anew not only to commit to providing the needed care my family deserves, but also to fine-tune the balance between this care and the other demands of ministry.

How Conflict Taught Me to Restructure Priorities

A distressing argument with my wife, Diana, opened my eyes to my neglectful behavior. Nonetheless, I found it hard to accept this confrontation as necessary to bring about needed changes.

"Bitching," says psychologist Arch Hart, "gives valuable information."[1] The argument with Diana gave me valuable information, and I was forced to pay attention to problems that had put our family off balance. Here is what happened.

The quarrel which opened my eyes concerned an insane schedule tied to the demands of a bivocational ministry. I was working as a sales representative, and the obligations of this job took me out of town three or more days per week. Diana was left at home with the children, the church, and our bookstore business.

One stressful morning, my wife boiled over with anger and frustration:

> Dan, you go out on the road for two or three days, and the load is doubled for me at home. I have to take calls for the church; I run the bookstore we have started, and on top of all this stress, the children come home and ask me, "Where is Dad? Where is Dad?!"

Diana continued:

> And I am asking, "Where is my *husband*!?" You are gone on your sales job for three or more days, and then you come home and throw your energies into the church and bookstore. When is there time for us? Do you not understand? I and the children need you! We are tired of being left alone!

Diana's words cut deeply, and I snapped back:

> Just a minute, Dear! I give you and the children time. I do not leave you or them out. Besides, we agreed sales work would give time, money, and flexibility that would not be possible with a low-paying job in our rural community.

"That may be so," Diana replied, "but look, the plan is not working. You do not bring in enough commissions to justify the time you spend away from us. In addition, the motel and auto expenses are too high. I am sorry, but I am tired of paying the price so you can go out and chase your windmills!"

At this point, I exploded:

> Diana! I am not chasing windmills! I don't want to be swallowed up by poverty. I am doing this to provide for the family in our difficult and unusual circumstances. Don't you understand?

Diana's eyes brimmed with tears. She said, "I know what you are trying to do, but it is not working. I want my husband, and the children want their dad."

*   *   *

As I said, the argument had a life-changing outcome. Diana and the children were suffering. Consequently, I was compelled to restructure my priorities.

I resigned from my church position, which by its nature forced the overextension of my time and my absence from our home. We then accepted a new ministry assignment that, although bivocational, made it possible to find a better-paying job close to home. With traveling and unnecessary stress eliminated, I could concentrate on paying attention to family life and balancing it properly with ministry.

When editing the initial draft of this chapter, I noticed my almost automatic use of the phrase "paying attention" when referring to the pressure created by this family crisis. As a result, I was reminded of what Scott Peck defined as love:

> The principal form that the work of love takes is attention. When we love one another, we give him or her our attention; we attend to that person's growth. When we love ourselves, we attend to our own growth. When we attend to someone, we are caring for that person.[2]

HAZARDS OF NEGLECT

Fortunately, I discovered my problem of family neglect before I lost my wife and children. Nevertheless, a question persists: How is it that male pastors can so easily lay aside their families without knowing what is happening or without giving the abandonment a second thought? Female pastors do not appear to have the same problem. Here are some possible reasons for this puzzle.

Is this true?

An Inadequate Model of Ministry

The historical model for the male "superpastor" has provided little or no space for the family. This is not to say a church does not want a pastor's family. On the contrary, evangelical churches, which are non-Catholic, almost always insist a male pastor come packaged with a family.

Concurrently, churches that do not hold the tradition of a celibate priesthood frequently view single male pastors with suspicion. The first concern is sexual orientation: "Why is he not married? Is he gay?" The second concern is for children. Parishioners think to themselves and out loud, "Didn't *60 Minutes* just do an exposé on child-molesting priests? How can we trust any unmarried male minister to keep his hands off of our children?" Finally, if the single male minister is straight and is not a molester, he is still not free of the quandary. The parish continues to be anxious:

> OK, our pastor is not gay nor is he a molester. That means he is normal. If that is the case, the unattached females in our midst are fair game. The man is single, and he must be looking. Who can trust him with our maidens?!

Given these common, though not often expressed fears, the family of a male minister removes these pressures and relieves the accompanying anxiety often felt by the congregation. However, too many of these "relieved" congregations fail to take the next step by giving the pastor's family identity and respect. What happens instead is the pastor's family becomes nothing more than a necessary appendage that the congregation feels free to exploit, along with the time and talent of the pastor.

This injustice is played out in churches everywhere. For example, Pastor Jones accepts the call to First Church, and as a consequence, Mrs. Jones is expected to play the piano, direct children's church, baby-sit without advance notice, and allow anyone to drop in at her home, day or night, with no invitation. In addition to these pressures, Mrs. Jones must be sure that she keeps a clean house and that her children behave like saints.

James Street writes intensely of this dilemma and injustice in the novel *The Gauntlet.* The heroes, Pastor London Wingo and his wife, Kathie, unleash inhibited emotions when anger and frustration boil over:

> He [London Wingo] sat on the bed by her and touched her. "Kathie—"
>
> Then she sat up in bed and the tears dried in her eyes . . . "I hate it all," she said. "Do you hear me, London Wingo? I hate it!"
>
> ". . . Savages! That's what they are. Filthy savages mouthing homage to their God of ignorance."
>
> "And those vicious old hens. Tama and Josie have fangs. . . . It's my baby, and Josie tried to tell me what to do. I can't even have my own name. This is not a home. It's a goldfish bowl. Do this, do that. Don't wear that. Do! Do! Don't! Don't! Don't! **DON'T!** To hell with them, London Wingo!"[3]

The Codependent Workaholic

The image of the codependent workaholic is at the heart of a flawed model for a pastor, and this image can be held either by the congregation or the pastor himself. There are many misconceptions inherent in this view. Besides offering his family as sacrificial lambs, the superpastor:

- does not need sleep;
- never makes mistakes;
- is available to everybody all the time;
- can live without money;
- has telepathic powers (when someone feels bad, superpastor can somehow magically show up at just the right time and make his/her day without being told a thing);

- can solve all problems and church conflicts;
- preaches convicting[4] sermons without making anyone upset;
- never gets tired;
- never gets angry;
- never gets sick;
- keeps everybody happy; and
- does not have to care for his family.

These expectations are not only unrealistic, they are dysfunctional. A pastor who meets all of these expectations becomes a codependent.

What is codependency? The meaning is hard to pin down according to author Melody Beattie. Nonetheless, she offers this definition in her book *Codependent No More:* "A codependent is one who has let another person's behavior affect him or her, and who is obsessed with controlling that person's behavior."[5] In addition, Phyllis Alsdurf offers these insights in her article "The Generic Disease": ". . . codependents are caretakers who are overcommitted and overinvolved in the lives of needy individuals."[6]

Codependency and its expressions of overcommitment and workaholism are considered addictive behaviors by doctors and psychologists in the field of recovery therapy. However, despite this assessment, these behaviors are held in high esteem by many contemporary churches. The codependent is the pathological expression of the pastor-hero myth:

- "I have such a good pastor; he is so self-sacrificing."
- "My pastor spent weeks with me in the hospital. He came every day and sat at my bedside."
- "I can call my pastor any time, day or night. He will drop anything he is doing, even time with his family, just to help me when I am in trouble."

The same myth prevails for the heroic pastor's wife:

- "Mrs. Pastor is so faithful. She will take anybody's Sunday school class if they don't show up to teach."

- "Mrs. Pastor plays the piano beautifully, and the good thing about it is she plays for free. How about that! We get two for the price of one."
- "Mrs. Pastor will play hostess anytime we go visit her home—even at a moment's notice. Her house is always spotless, and she makes such good refreshments."

I believe the notion of superpastor mirrors the misconception of God on call: a genie in a lamp. Some individuals pay no attention to spiritual matters until there is trouble. In a knee-jerk reaction to trouble, these same persons run to God as if to a genie in a lamp, pleading to God to bail them out. The purpose of the supplications is to fix a problem so life will be comfortable again. This is "God in the foxhole" mentality.

Unfortunately, "God in the foxhole" can quickly become "pastor in the foxhole"—for the desperate. The codependent pastor-hero becomes an "ace in the hole"—an easy touch for a quick fix in tough times. This seductive model of the ideal minister who represents a "genie god" reflects the state of our social dysfunction and spiritual poverty.

In the foregoing scenario, congregations may collectively assume the role of a raging alcoholic as each member conspires to manipulate the minister. The dysfunctional pastor responds to this addictive acting out by attempting to manage and control his flock's unpredictable behavior. The result is pastor burnout.

Despite the pathological nature of the aforementioned church relationships, some will quote scripture to validate the pastor-hero/codependent model. Luke 14:26 is a frequently used prooftext: "If anyone comes to me and does not hate his father and mother, his wife and children, his brothers and sisters—yes even his own life—he cannot be my disciple" (NIV).

Let us pause for a minute. This is as far into the scripture as some go to prove their point. "See," such persons will say, "the real pastor-hero leaves all for the sake of God's kingdom."

It appears to be true that the first part of this passage exhorts the faithful to desert possessions and family for the sake of the kingdom of God. Nonetheless, the interpretation and application of this excerpt is as diverse as the scholars who examine it. Some who look at the passage go no further than to declare a verbatim translation of the scripture that presupposes the faithful in Christ will give up everything, including family relationships, to do the will of God. However, William Barclay expresses a different point of view in interpreting this passage. He suggests that the verse is not to be taken literally.

> We must not take his words with cold, unimaginative literalness. Eastern language is always as vivid as the human mind can make it. When Jesus tells us to hate our nearest and dearest, he does not mean that literally. He means that no love in life can compare with the love we must bear to him.[7]

Further, the interpretation and application of any scripture necessarily takes into consideration the complete context of the New Testament. Within the contextual framework of the New Testament, one would be hard pressed to find justification for abandoning one's family and that family's needs to do the will of God. The unconditional love and commitment we give to Christ includes the love, care, and nurture of the wife and children who make up the male pastor's family.

Here are just a few examples of scriptures that illustrate how uncompromising love and commitment to Christ do not presuppose the abandonment of one's family.

1. Jesus was tested by the Pharisees in Matthew 19 with the question, "Is it lawful for a man to divorce his wife for any and every reason?" (Matthew 19:3, NIV). Jesus (who realized that a Jewish woman had virtually no legal rights in divorce[8]) replied, "Haven't you read . . . that at the beginning the Creator 'made them male and female,' and said, 'For this reason a man will leave his father and mother and be united to his wife, and the two will become one flesh'? So they are no longer two, but one. Therefore what God has joined together let not man separate" (Matthew 19:4-5, NIV). Jesus appears not only to express the oneness of a man and woman in marriage, but Jesus also appears to advocate for the protection and dignity of the woman who was considered the property of the man she married.[9]

2. Parallel to the above passage, Ephesians 5 states the following: "Husbands, love your wives just as Christ loved the church . . . husbands ought to love their wives as their own bodies. He who loves his wife loves himself. After all, no one ever hated his own body . . ." (Ephesians 5:25-29, NIV).

3. Regarding the nurture of children, Jesus says in Matthew 19, "Let the little children come to me, and do not hinder them, for the kingdom of heaven belongs to such as these" (Matthew 19:14, NIV). Although the passage specifically describes Jesus' willingness to receive children, the larger implication is that the children (who experience oppression as do women) are entitled to time and attention befitting them as possessors of the kingdom of heaven.[10]

4. Parallel to the above passage, Ephesians 6:4 and Colossians 3:21 give these charges to fathers: "Fathers do not provoke your children to anger, but bring them up in discipline and instruction of the Lord" (Ephesians 6:4, RSV). "Fathers, do not embitter your children, or they will become discouraged" (Colossians 3:21, NIV). The point here is that the children not only deserve but need the time and attention of both parents, especially the father. The pursuit of a pastor toward his calling to the exclusion of his children and their needs has created an almost ubiquitous resentment of preachers' children toward their fathers. When they become adults, many grieve the loss of the time they never had with their pastor dads.[11]

5. 1 Timothy 5:8 chides the economic neglect of an ill-provided family. Nevertheless, a metaphorical application of emotional neglect and neglect of presence is not a farfetched utilization of this scripture: "If anyone does not provide for his relatives, and especially his own family, he has disowned the faith and is worse than an unbeliever" (1 Timothy 5:8, RSV).

6. At least two scriptures in the New Testament appear to argue that if one were to accept a call to ministry that would adversely affect a family, such a person is encouraged not to marry and consequently avoid the future suffering a wife and children might experience in a difficult vocational pursuit. Paul makes reference to celibacy with this presupposition: "Now for the matters you wrote about: It is good for a man not to marry. . . . But those who marry face many troubles in this life, and I want to spare you this. . . . I would like you to be free from

concern. An unmarried man is concerned about the Lord's affairs—
how he can please the Lord. But a married man is concerned about the
affairs of this world—how he can please his wife—and his interests
are divided. . . . I am saying this for your own good, not to restrict you,
but that you may live in a right way in undivided devotion to the
Lord" (1 Corinthians 7:1, 28, 32-33, 35, NIV).[12] Concurrently, Jesus
makes this statement in Matthew 19: "Not everyone can accept this
word, but only to those to whom it has been given. For some are
eunuchs because they were born that way; others were made that
way by men; and others have renounced marriage because of the
kingdom of heaven. The one who can accept this should accept it"
(Matthew 19: 11-12, NIV).[13]

These are just a few of the contextual distinctives of the New
Testament used to explain that giving one's total love and commitment to Christ does not mean a literal abandonment of the family.

Furthermore, though feminist theology does not encompass the
scope of this writing, this archetype of liberation theology is seeking to
re-examine traditional religious views of the family from the perspective of the woman as interpreter. Lee McGee states:

> Feminist thought has centered on the issue of mutuality of
> partnerships, and this has revealed the many oppressive and
> hierarchical dimensions of marriage as a social institution . . .
> Feminist theologians and pastors are actively working to probe
> and address the changing concepts of relationship in family
> and society. Work to reassert an ethic of mutuality and ac-
> countability is vital.[14]

All things considered, the new model I propose in this book
addresses the issues of mutuality and accountability in the male
pastor's relationship with his wife and children.

TOWARD A NEW MODEL OF MINISTRY

In the pages ahead, we tell our story as a pastor's family. We
candidly share our history (the good and the bad) with a hope that our
sufferings and insights will be windows to change. The change we
envision has four components:

1. A restructured model of ministry;
2. The improved physical/emotional/spiritual health of pastors' families everywhere;
3. The improved health of the congregational family and the families within the congregation; and
4. Increased awareness of addictive/pathological hazards in family/church/society relationships with strategies for recovery.

Join us in this exploration as Diana begins by telling her story.

Chapter 2

The Experience
of Being a Pastor's Wife

Diana's experience as a pastor's wife has been, in part, a story about struggle and frustration in coping with a flawed model of ministry. When I discussed with Diana the formal preparation of this portion of our narrative, she said, "I get very angry when I go over this history. The memory of the bad experiences is very painful. Please don't ask me to write the story directly. I have verbally expressed my deep feelings. You complete the job of putting my story into print."

Consequently, I will tell Diana's story.

HISTORY AND CRISIS

The Setting

The beginning of this story is set in the unique timeframe that we both share. I am a pre-baby boomer; I was born in 1943, and at one time, our generation was called the War Baby Generation. Diana was born in 1948 so she is considered a "baby boomer." Notwithstanding, our respective "settings in time" parallel major cultural changes that occurred during and after World War II. Particularly, attitudes toward the role of women underwent significant changes, and we found ourselves living on both sides of this cultural shift.

Our respective wartime and postwar families were, at least outwardly, the *Ozzie and Harriet/Leave It to Beaver* models. Both of our mothers were housewives who believed the appropriate woman's role was to be the primary caregiver for children and an emotional and physical support to the husband/father. Our families were patriarchal structures in which the goals and dreams of the male head took precedence over the dreams and desires of any other family member.

This patriarchal structure was especially prominent in Diana's family. Diana's family defined the role of women as that of servants who attended to male needs and demands. Her mother attended to every need of the husband/father. This father-dominated family sculpture with specifically defined female roles sparked an early conflict in our marriage.

Even though my own family of origin was traditional, the male-female roles were not rigid. I helped my mother change my younger brothers' diapers, I learned to cook, and I also helped with housework. Diana's family considered these chores to be female responsibilities, and her father and brothers considered males who did what they called "women's work" unmanly.

Because of her family background, Diana became distressed when she discovered, shortly after our marriage, that I liked to cook. I further upset her when I explained that I didn't expect her to serve all the meals or do all the housework. Diana frequently expressed feelings of displacement in those early years. She said, "If you do not want me to cook your meals or wash your clothes, what *do* you want from me? After all, I am your wife!"

Despite these stressful beginnings, we both became comfortable with sharing housekeeping chores. Diana has accepted my involvement, and she no longer feels displaced.

However, despite my superficial effort to be a progressive and caring husband, Diana still suffered subtle sex discrimination and patriarchal abuse. The reason for this abuse can be traced to the social values of our past. The mistreatment I perpetrated was the demand that my goals and dreams as a husband/father come first. No one else in the family unit had comparable privilege. Here is how this ghost of an older social order caused my wife to suffer.

Male Dominance and Family Goals

Our families of origin in an older social order labeled the father as the breadwinner. Typically, these families followed the father/husband as he followed his career. The wife/mother was primarily a homemaker; any work done by the wife/mother outside the home was understood to be temporary and was abandoned when the role of homemaker became jeopardized.

In contrast to this model from the past, Diana and I have both worked throughout our marriage. I have never been the sole provider. Nevertheless, I still insisted that my career plans and goals come first. My decision to enter seminary is a case in point.

First, let me clarify that neither Diana nor my children were against these plans to enter ministry; I received full support. Notwithstanding, the family paid a dear price, and my wife experienced the greatest loss.

What Diana lost was the time and attention of her husband to other lovers. These paramours were educational achievement, success, and personal growth. The goals in themselves are not wrong. However, when you as the husband/father are the only one benefiting, these dreams become whores. This is precisely the focus of the deep hurt my wife still feels and the reason it is so painful for her to tell her story.

The Pressure of Seminary Years

I took on the challenge of seminary with the determination to be a high achiever. We moved close to the campus, and I took a full course load every semester. Also, I worked two jobs to ensure we had adequate income.[1] Thus, in addition to regular classwork, I was working fifty-plus hours a week outside of school, day and night.

Yes, I achieved my goals. I maintained a 3.0 grade average through all three years of seminary, and I graduated on time. Nevertheless, my wife had no husband and the children had no father during these years.

Diana reflects bitterly on those years: "Those days were hell for me, and the way you achieved your goals was not fair to either me or the children."

This abuse is even more injurious because it is is a given in the structure of seminary preparation. The suffering family is the inevitable price for the training of the minister. The faithful wife becomes the linchpin that makes the education of the male minister possible. The seminary wife is expected to care for children, hold the family together, and take an extra job so the husband can attend his classes and fulfill his dreams. Thus, the structures of ministerial training, as I experienced them, expect the wife to pay the heaviest price for the minister's education.

Diana attempted to get something out of the experience. She started working for a degree in music at the same school I was attending. However, she chose to quit because, as she put it, "I can't go to school, work as a nurse thirty hours a week, and provide care for the children."

Two things now disturb me when I look back to graduation. First, a tongue-in-cheek, backhanded compliment was inadvertently paid to seminary wives. Each wife got a PHT diploma. The wife's degree title was "Putting Husband Through." This happened fifteen years ago, but I contend this supposedly humorous diploma was actually a blatant rubber stamp of sexism and exploitation of the pastor's wife.

Women attended Golden Gate Seminary and graduated with the same degree as the men. However, opportunities for employment were severely limited. The academic setting in a Southern Baptist seminary is different from the worldview of most Southern Baptist Churches, which are largely conservative and resist inviting women to take nontraditional roles as pastors and church leaders.

Second, I remember speaking with one of my seminary professors about the wear and tear inflicted on families during the years a husband/father attends seminary. The professor replied, "Someone has to pay the price." I walked away musing, "Why does it have to be the wife?"

The First Six Years in a Church

Following seminary graduation, we sought placement in our first church. We accepted a call, and this first pastorate almost destroyed our marriage.

Because money was scarce and problems were abundant, Diana and I ended up with the same insane schedule and lifestyle we had experienced in seminary. I pastored the church as a bivocational minister in which part of my income was obtained through secular work. I opened a bookstore, and I went into business as an independent sales representative, selling gifts and bakery supplies.

Once again, Diana got stuck with the cleanup. I would leave town at 5:00 a.m. and be gone three or four days. She cared for the children almost as a single parent; Diana readied them for school, dealt with their crises, and generally held the household together.

In addition, my wife ran our bookstore when I was on the road and she took all the calls for the church and handled the flak and problems while I was out of town. She did this with no pay or title.

As a result, our lives became more unmanageable for two reasons:

1. I wasn't paying attention to what was going on.
2. The social/religious structure we worked under encouraged an unspoken exploitation of a pastor's wife.

I believe God's sheer grace and Diana's deep love are what saved our marriage. Nevertheless, our past holds painful memories, and our present discloses serious challenges.

You now know something of our history; here, then, is Diana's narrative.

DIANA'S STORY

I have always dreamed of being a pastor's wife, but now I do not know. Some people have envied my role as a minister's wife because I have a "spiritual" husband. Many women I have met wish their husbands were as spiritually sensitive. This is what I tell them: "Forget about marrying a prince. If you marry a prince, you have to clean up after the horse."

I guess this has been the hardest thing for me as a pastor's wife. I have been the mop-up lady for Dan's dreams. I do not begrudge my husband's dreams, but I have a life too, and I have had to lay aside my dreams so my husband could have his.

This starts with the children. A mother no longer has a life of her own once the children come along. A mother simply has to learn to give up control over her time and forgo her desires because the children require it. Men do not understand this. They do not have to sacrifice in the same way a mother does. Men do lots of playing and do not adjust to accommodating to the needs of others.

I have embraced my role, willingly, as a mother. I love my children, and I feel a tremendous responsibility to give them proper care and to nurture them. What I did not envision was raising children alone, and this is what has angered me.

First, Dan was busy in seminary, and then he threw himself into the ministry and his outside work. He was gone too much. He was not there for me as a husband and lover. I felt as if I was a single parent, widow, and divorcée all rolled into one.

I resented not only being single-handedly responsible for the children, but also for having to carry the load of the church and the bookstore when he was out of town. This was a workload I didn't ask for, and I almost left.

My children took away the control of my time; my husband did too. I felt not only neglected but abandoned as well.

What further makes me angry is that the church too often expects the unpaid, mop-up, pastor's wife to be part of the deal when the husband is hired. That is wrong. I do not believe I am just an extension of my husband's ministry. I am a person in my own right, and this brings up another pet peeve.

Frequently in social/religious gatherings, people forget my name. They only remember me as an appendage of the pastor: "That is the pastor's wife. . . . That is Dan's wife." Hey! I am not just the pastor's wife! I have a name. I am Diana. I too am a person, and I have an identity apart from my husband. I want to be known for who I am: I am a nurse. I love to knit. I love fabrics. I also dream of becoming a great pianist.

There is another problem associated with my position: when you are a pastor's wife, who is *your* pastor? I have not really had a pastor since we have been in the ministry. When your husband is the church pastor, it is difficult for him to be your pastor. Who helps *us* with *our* marriage? Sometimes, I wish I went to a different church; I need a pastor too. At times, I truly feel alone and abandoned.

THE OUTCOME OF CRISIS

Someone once defined crisis as a "dangerous opportunity." Such an opportunity came to us, unexpectedly, in the spring of 1988.

Diana and I attended a DMin seminar at Fuller Seminary, which was conducted by psychologist Arch Hart. The title of the seminar was "The Minister's Personal Growth and Skill Development Workshop." Through insights presented and the intervention facilitated by Dr. Hart, I was forced to face critical issues in our relationship that needed healing and restructuring. This is the revelation that I discussed in the opening chapter, and this was the turning point of our marriage and ministry.

I have come to realize that the healing of past sins and imbalances will be an ongoing process. As such, we will be fine-tuning our relationship for the rest of our years together. Nonetheless, here is the progress we have made.

1. The success and career of the pastor/husband/father is no longer the solitary goal of our family; Diana is now getting her turn. The family focus is now on my wife's career and her education. Diana is now working toward her BSN, and she wants to become a nursing administrator.
2. My current role as a pastor/church planter approaches a better balance between attention to family versus the needs of ministry. The mix is still not perfect, but the stress-generating schedule is gone, and I am more aware of my wife's needs.
3. We have gotten in touch not only with our own histories before we became husband and wife, but also with our unique place in a society and denomination (American Baptist Churches, USA) that are seeking to change attitudes toward women. We both realize that it is no longer acceptable for the pastor's wife to be the unappreciated, unpaid linchpin of her husband's ministry. The pastor's wife has an identity apart from her pastor/husband, and she has the right to fulfill her own dreams.

Despite these insights and the increasing awareness of the need for social/religious change in relation to the pastor's family, the culture of the Protestant Christian community continues to be shackled with a script from the past. On the one hand, more leaders within the Protestant Christian community have recognized the need for structural change and the liberation of the pastor's wife and women in general from sex-discriminating roles in the church. On the other hand, the pastor's wife continues to be the mop-up lady and second-class citizen in too many local churches.

I look forward to the end of spousal abuse of the pastor's wife that is supported by structures and attitudes within the church and Christian community. Toward this end, Chapter 3 analyzes gender discrimination as it affects the minister's wife.

Chapter 3

Who Is Going to Make the Coffee?

Diana works full-time as a director of nurses for a convalescent hospital. She works at least fifty hours a week. This work schedule has been typical for Diana for most of our marriage. Consequently, one might think my wife should easily ignore the pressure placed upon her to volunteer for the seemingly endless supply of unfilled jobs in church. Unfortunately, this has not been her experience. Although Diana has declined to be the mop-up lady, she has said no with considerable guilt. I believe this guilt is imposed upon the pastor's wife by the unspoken sentiment that the role of a minister's spouse is to work side by side with her pastor/husband regardless of the hours she may work in her own career. This is a problem of gender bias and inappropriate expectations in modern Protestant culture.

ROLE REVERSAL

Consider for a moment if we reversed roles. Suppose Diana was the pastor, and I was the spouse. How would attitudes change when the supporting spouse is male? Conceivably, few congregations would pressure me as a pastor's husband to volunteer for mop-up chores in the church with the same zeal exerted to recruit the pastor's wife. Female pastors are as yet an emerging minority in the more conservative, evangelical churches. Nonetheless, current attitudes appear to allow the pastor's husband more freedom to determine his involvement in his wife's church than the wife of a pastor is allowed in a similar situation.

Thus, the male minister's spouse is more likely to be enslaved as a congregation's Cinderella while the female minister's spouse will likely live as a prince. The question then is: Why does this oppression of the minister's wife persist when we in the 1990s are supposedly part of a decade that is allowing women greater justice and self-determination? This is a perplexing problem. The churches in our society should be the leaders and modelers of equal status for every person regardless of gender. Unfortunately, traditional and oppressive attitudes persist.

As recently as 1990, I applied for a pastoral position in an established church that was knowledgeable of the efforts of the larger Christian community to affirm a more equal position of women within the church and to correct practices that foster gender oppression. Nonetheless, questions at the beginning of this candidacy interview focused on my wife. She was immediately asked to make extensive volunteer commitments as a condition of our acceptance by this congregation. Diana would not make these commitments, and I was withdrawn from consideration. The pulpit committee stated that they declined my candidacy because this congregation didn't want a "chalkboard" preacher (whatever that meant). However, Diana intuitively surmised the rejection was linked to her refusal to play the role this church demanded of its future pastor's wife.

The reasons for this pervasive gender abuse of the minister's wife could be linked to inconsistent attitudes toward women in the broader culture.

THE PASTOR'S WIFE AS CARETAKER

Journalist Jon Tevlin asserts that maybe we have not come as far as we think when it comes to treatment of women in our culture. In his article, "Why Women Are Mad as Hell," he describes 1991 as a year in which pop culture affirms justice for oppressed females through forums such as the movie *Thelma and Louise*. On the other hand, during this same year, the nation watched the "appalling treatment" of Anita Hill by the Senate during the Clarence Thomas hearings. (The female victim once again becomes the accused.) Even in those discerning days, the Anita Hill case "evoked a phrase again and again from women across the country: *Men just don't get it.*"[1]

The problems in the Anita Hill incident can be extended to the dilemma of the pastor's wife; both men and women in certain congregations "still don't get it." Honestly, why *don't* we get it when it comes to oppression of the minister's wife?

In a 1980 survey, Loren Mead reflected that the pastor's wife in the predominantly male-led profession of clergy is frequently a victim of sexism and clericalism. In this survey, sixteen out of twenty clergy wives perceived themselves as treated like a "non-person" in their respective congregations. Ten out of the twenty felt like unpaid staff.[2]

In 1989, Jack Balswick cited a list of the most frequent complaints pastors' wives enumerated about their roles:

1. Not having a life apart from the church and living up to other members' expectations
2. Fighting feelings that I must be a certain type of person
3. People who feel I am a little more than human
4. Feeling that I'm always on display, that I can't be myself
5. The feeling of being under observation in all circumstances[3]

In addition, this "not getting it" may be what Edwin Friedman calls *homeostasis* and what Dennis Guernsey calls *morphostasis*.[4] These two terms refer to a general resistance that people and cultures have toward change. Even when something is perceived as bad (such as the exploitation of the pastor's wife), it is familiar and much less threatening than the unknown outcomes that result from change. Considering all of this, Jon Tevlin maintains that women have historically been society's caretakers. Thus, acknowledging the anger women are expressing about this role produces a cultural fear that women will no longer acquiesce to a caretaking role and will demand a more assertive place as leaders, innovators, and decision makers—that is, assuming roles that have been stereotypically identified as a man's domain.[5]

Similarly, I believe the institutional church harbors cultural fear when it comes to reevaluating traditional expectations for the pastor's wife because she is a caretaker in the eyes of many.

Carolyn Taylor Gutierrez describes presumptions of many congregations that the pastor's wife be a sort of "'holy noodle-head' . . . always-there-and-caring-first-for you."[6] If the pastor's wife dares to take a role different from this, she is considered "uppity" or "rectorine." Thus, there is likely a cultural fear that prevents congregations from relating more positively to the pastor's wife by giving her freedom and affirming her unique personhood.

This now brings us to the question posed in the chapter title, "Who Is Going to Make the Coffee?" An appendix to this question is another question: What does the role of the pastor's wife and gender discrimination have to do with the pastor's family, and why is so much time being spent on this subject?

The best answer to these questions comes when I reflect on our marriage. A considerable amount of the spousal conflict in my pastor's family has been over the issue of the abuse and exploitation of the pastor's wife. I am the main perpetrator, and the parish has followed on my heels because I permitted it.

As the primary antagonist, I put pressure on Diana to be something she wasn't and to perform the impossible because I also was afraid to initiate change. By the grace of God, we did not divorce, and the reason our marriage survived is credited to Diana's strength throughout her suffering. She was willing to insist and persist until I finally did get it.

What did I finally get? I got some ideas about change and justice for the pastor's wife. The following pages present these insights.

Allow the Pastor's Wife to Write Her Own Script

What is wrong with giving the minister's wife this freedom? The minister is allowed to respond to his calling as he understands it. Why should his wife be denied the same right? Let me illustrate from our experience.

Diana is a very private person with the gift of caring and intercession. She needs her space and views her home as a sanctuary from the outside world. I am exactly the opposite. I am a gregarious and social person, and I love to have people around. Concurrently, many congregations believe a gregarious minister to be an entitlement and some of these same congregations see the parsonage as an extension of the church fellowship hall. Consequently, the assumption persists that the good minister will turn his parsonage into Grand Central Station and make it the staging area for a perpetual feast and spiritual party.

My wife said, "No! I don't want my house to be Grand Central Station. I want the sanctuary of my home so I can be refreshed and attain the time I need to be alone with you and the children. If the congregation doesn't like this, they will need to learn to adjust. I know what my limits are."

Such a separation of home and church is an absolute necessity for my wife's survival and preservation of her identity. Hence, our script is written: the parsonage is *not* an extension of the church fellowship hall.

This decision to make our residence a private sanctuary is not always well-received by every member of the congregation nor every official in the denomination. Nevertheless, the assurance of a set-apart and *private* home life allows Diana to function without resentment and to release her spiritual gifts of intercession and one-on-one ministry with those who experience pain and suffering. This bigger picture of my wife's unique calling more appropriately serves the will of God and the church than would turn the home into the congregation's watering hole.

Peter Wagner, in a seminar on church growth, discussed the operation of spiritual gifts, and the subject came up about pastors' wives who want homes as sanctuaries versus meeting halls. Wagner replied this way:

> I believe hospitality is a spiritual gift, and I believe it is wrong to force somebody to function in an area to which they have not been called. A wife should not be forced to function in the gift of hospitality if that is not her calling.[7]

I understand this process of allowing persons within the pastor's family to set their own limits to be healthy and ultimately beneficial to the church. Lee and Balswick call this process *differentiation*. Although differentiation requires some negotiation and compromise, the process allows an individual to help create the framework and boundaries of a social situation so that he/she will have some sense of control and not feel exploited. The key element in differentiation is the ability of an individual to maintain a distinctive identity.[8]

Slay the Sacred Cows

In support of the previous discussion, Roy Oswald advocates challenging traditional congregational norms in open discussion when it relates to expectations for the pastor's wife. He suspects few congregations raise the issue for consideration. As a result, according to Oswald, "Congregations rob themselves of the opportunities to move into positions of greater health."[9]

Oswald further sees the failure to negotiate the pastor's wife's role as the loss of a valuable resource—her.

> Clergy wives are usually a talented, creative, dedicated group of Christians. When they are relegated to being "non-persons," when their point of view is never taken seriously . . . the church as a whole is diminished.
>
> If in any way their lives are made miserable through attitudes and actions on behalf of church members, that negative energy spills over and adversely affects the parish's life.[10]

Oswald also says that there is a direct correlation between healthy parishes and healthy attitudes toward both the pastor and the spouse.

SUMMARY

Diana has the right as a human being to the same freedoms as I have. Her position as a pastor's wife should not hinder these freedoms. She has the right to equality (Galatians 3:28), autonomy (Galatians 5:1), and the right of self-determination (1 Corinthians 2:10-16). The direction of movement of the Holy Spirit in these days appears to clarify through the example of Christ and the preaching of Paul that restrictions of personal freedom and identity through gender bias (especially as it relates to the role of the pastor's wife) should be abolished. Such biases have been wrong and hurtful throughout the history of the church. A fresh understanding of gender roles, especially in marriage, is one of mutuality.

John Howell quotes Samuel Southard on this subject:

> A plan for new lifestyles must balance commitment to a mate with fulfillment of the self. More specifically, there must be equality of the sexes. Men and women must be intimate friends who find in each other the qualities they enjoy in themselves. Mutual admiration is mixed with sexual affection and social responsibility. The result is a formula: Like the one you love.[11]

John Howell also cites Arthur Rouner, who said agape love "is letting someone else's life be more important than your own."[12]

I am trying to learn to express this kind of love to my wife and children, who are part of this pastor's family. So, who is going to make the coffee? If my wife wants to, that is OK. However, if this symbolic "making of coffee" becomes an issue of restricted freedom and gender bias against my wife as a woman, I as the male will pour and serve.

In the next chapter, you will have the opportunity to read my children's candid assessments on life as "PKs" (preacher's kids). Then in the subsequent chapter, we explore biblical mandates for the pastor to care for his family.

SECTION II:
THE PASTOR AND HIS CHILDREN

Chapter 4

My PKs: Their Stories

We gave our son, Daniel Aaron, a fly-tying kit for Christmas when he was ten. We did not know at the time that this gift would shape his future.

This gift was fitting for Danny because we were pastoring a church which was in a California coastal village that fronted on one of the best-known steelhead trout rivers in California and the world. Danny's boyhood playground was this river.

I said the fly-tying kit shaped my son's destiny. The kit did so because through the discovery of this hobby Danny developed a passion for fly-fishing and concurrently a passion for the outdoors. He developed an interest in the conservation of wilderness and wild rivers as well as an aspiration to live his life as close to nature as possible.

During my son's childhood and adolescence, he became acquainted with world-famous fly fishermen. He befriended these men when he met them on the river. Danny sought their wisdom and gleaned sophisticated tips that polished his craft. Further, Danny learned about all the great fly-fishing rivers of North America and the world. In addition, he has become an expert on the natural history not only of steelhead and other trout, but also of the multitude of insects upon which these fish feed. Dan Aaron can create a lure out of thread and feathers that looks exactly like a caddis fly or a mayfly and which a steelhead or other trout cannot resist. This talent, coupled with the professional skill he possesses with a fly rod, has helped my son become a world-class angler.

Thus, you may understand why the film and story *A River Runs Through It* snagged more than just my passing interest. The opening lines of this book clarify the uncanny resemblance between the childhood setting of my son's life and the similar family setting depicted in *A River Runs Through It:*

> In our family, there was no clear line between religion and fly fishing. We lived at the junction of great trout rivers in western Montana, and our father was a Presbyterian minister and a fly fisherman who tied his own flies and taught others. He told us about Christ's disciples being fishermen, and we were left to assume, as my brother and I did, that all first-class fishermen on the Sea of Galilee were fly fishermen and that John, the favorite, was a dry-fly fisherman.[1]

I am not a fly fisherman, and my son has a sister, not a brother. Nevertheless, much of *A River Runs Through It* parallels life experiences Danny and I have shared. I asked Danny, "What did you think about the movie?"

He told me straight away, "I didn't like it, Dad, because it hit too close to home."

The resultant dialogue we had together concerning this story impressed upon me the ambivalence my son experienced growing up as a PK. The reason Danny said he was uncomfortable with *A River Runs Through It* lies in the experiences of the minister's two sons who were in the story: Norman and Paul MacLean.

Danny said, "I am like them both, and that bothers me. Also, the family in the movie is so close to ours that I just didn't like watching it."

Norman and Paul MacLean, PKs in *A River Runs Through It,* spent their lives attempting to adjust to a real world that was at odds with the world of their minister/father and often at odds with who they were as developing human beings.

The world of the minister/father was one of piety, justice, discipline, ethical values, and distance from life in secular culture. Reverend MacLean's world just did not seem real or adaptable to the world his sons experienced.

The world Paul and Norman MacLean saw and experienced was one where drunks fought bloody fights in the streets. The world they saw was a world of brothels, gambling, drunkenness, dishonest people, broken promises, and chaotic lives lived without discipline.

There was a wide gulf between the life of the minister's family and the real world of Montana in the early twentieth-century.

The two boys attempted to adjust to the disharmony of these worlds in disparate ways. Paul became a newspaper reporter in Helena, and he followed his compulsion for wild living, alcohol, and gambling. Norman chose a more stable route that included marriage, a stint with the forest service, and eventually a college teaching career.

I see that Paul and Norman MacLean are archetypes of alter egos that live in every PK. Norman was the respectable model while Paul was the rebel. I understand my son's dicomfort, for he has told me more than once of the battles that have raged within his own being as to how he wants to live and how he should live. Dan Aaron understands that he is Norman and Paul at the same time, and likewise, he struggles with the incompatibility of the Norman-Paul (Jekyll and Hyde) mix that is inside him and that he is trying to sort out.

Notwithstanding, Dan Aaron's greatest anger toward me as his minister/father is that I did not prepare him to face the *real* world through which he has had to suffer. Similar to Norman and Paul in *A River Runs Through It,* my son has seen me as a minister/father who is out of touch with life as he has had to live it. Here is Dan's story.

MY LIFE AS A PREACHER'S CHILD: DANIEL AARON LANGFORD

(Note: My son is now twenty-five years old, and his story is recorded exactly as he wrote it in 1993.)

There are a few things I can say about my life as a preacher's child that are cut and dried.

The good things:

1. I learned a lot about the way people in a church congregation act toward one another and their pastor. This has helped me to better understand people in general.
2. I was taught good Christian values as a child, but I misunderstood them at the time. Those same values I misunderstood are the ones I try to live by today.

3. I learned that there are a lot of people hurting, but I also learned no matter how bad different situations get, and no matter who the people are, people's problems all hurt the same. They just handle their pain differently.

The rest of my feelings are a mixture of both good and bad.

To start out, I think everybody older than myself in my dad's congregation felt it was their responsibility to act as my parents whenever my parents weren't around. They were constantly telling me how I should act. Even if their own children behaved outrageously, they would tell me how they felt a preacher's son should conduct himself.

I felt then and still feel now that every person in my father's congregation knew everything that happened to me. Every waking hour of the day, good or bad, they knew. The biggest factor was because my parents talked too much. I can't blame them. They trust everybody.

My parents can't see a person's bad qualities until that person or persons have severely hurt them. They (my parents) regularly told other people stories about our personal family life. In turn, the people whom they told retold over and over these stories to many different ears.

I believe my parents made a small but deadly mistake by being so open to so many different people. I have learned from this. I strive to avoid being the source of my own gossip. This creates less of a chance for me to become angry. In turn, the people who love to gossip have a better chance of keeping their face in the same arrangement.

The geographical area we lived in [my son's home during childhood and early adolescence] I felt at the time was normal. But since that time, I have not been in an area that had so few Christians. This made it hard on me as a preacher's son attending the area's public schools. I never felt comfortable telling people I was a preacher's son. When I did so, more times than not, I was ridiculed.

My father and mother never taught me anything but to be kind to people. In the real world, at least my part of it, this does not always work. When a person hits, you hit back. This is a concept (system of values) that at first I knew nothing about. This caused me to become confused.

Since our church represented a small minority in this area, I dropped God and tried to fit in with people who knew nothing about

God or hated everything about Him. My parents would not allow me to associate with these peers in any place but school. This caused a rift between my relationship with them and a bigger one between myself and God.

When I was seventeen, I moved with my parents to a larger urban area; we lived with my grandmother. My parents moved again to another community before I finished high school, so I stayed behind with my grandmother.

During this time, I did whatever I wanted whenever I wanted. I was always at parties and constantly getting into fights. I hated my father and mother for not teaching me anything but kindness. I was learning to fight the hard way, but I loved every minute of it.

I started to look down on my father because he never did anything I felt was manly. I felt it was my father's fault (he didn't teach me to fight) that I was only just now beginning to get respect for my so-called manly skills. Also, if I had a fight in which I or my friends felt I had performed inadequately, I would always blame my father.

Fortunately, I lived close to my mother's older brother, who was also a pastor. My uncle has the same temperament as I do, which has helped me greatly. My uncle is a veteran of many fights, and he has taught me much of his skill. He taught me how to fight on the streets and win. When my ego took over, and I became very cocky, he taught me that there are other ways to fight a person. These are ways that don't cause the other person pain. This has been a hard lesson to learn. My uncle said, "If what a person says will not matter to you in five years, it is not worth fighting over."

I have come to realize, through my uncle's help and discovering wisdom for myself, this simple fact: The best man is not always the strongest physically, but the one who makes the wisest judgment in dealing with a rough situation. This understanding has given me a new respect for my father—a respect I should have had all along. I have also learned that God controls my life, and that I owe him the best of my love and respect.

I believe my father is a great man. During his period as pastor at the congregation I mentioned, he dealt with some weak and evil people. These people used him for all his pastoral services but gave nothing in return. If these same people went to a psychiatrist as many times as they came to my father, they would have had to mortgage their homes to pay their bills. Even though our family struggled (financially) month by month, sometimes day by day, my father gave these people nothing but compassion.

As a child, I didn't respect or understand this. However, I now realize it took more courage to care for these people as my father did than it would to beat them to a bloody pulp, as I would be inclined to do. Someday I hope I can be as strong as my father.

I have learned that church life, as well as any other part of a person's life, is mostly a series of battles. There are more ways than one to fight these very different battles. I plan to use what my parents, my uncle, and my grandmother have taught me. I also plan to use what I have learned, and I will learn to teach my future children. I am praying that they will be wiser than I, and stronger Christians, so they can hopefully win all their battles.

MY REFLECTIONS ON DAN AARON'S AND DEANNA'S STORIES

Dan Aaron

Before my son wrote the story you just read, we went through a very intense period of conflict in our relationship. Dan Aaron savagely expressed the anger he felt because of my failure to equip him to face the physical violence and macho code of his world.

I explained to Dan Aaron that fighting was also a part of my life as a child, but I hated all that was connected with this choice. My decision was to walk away from physical violence simply because I abhorred it. I felt I did not have to prove myself with my fists, and I didn't care what people thought.

At the same time, I did not grow up as a preacher's son, nor did I grow up in the 1980s. Thus, I realize that the options I was able to choose from to resolve conflict and avoid violence may not be choices available to my son.

When Dan Aaron first expressed his disappointment that I didn't prepare him to survive in his world, I pleaded "no contest" to him.

His world is indeed foreign to me, and it is a world for which I have provided ineffective guidance and tools for survival. Thus, my son's Uncle Dean has been a provision of God's grace. He knows Dan Aaron's world, and he has been able to empower Dan with survival skills.

Further, the previous assessment of Dan Aaron's view of parental inadequacy is different from my view of failure as a parent. I perceived that my major shortcoming as a father was not spending enough time with my children. My son placed this inadequacy much further down his list. As just mentioned, Dan Aaron's major complaint was my failure to prepare him to fight in the real world. These differences concerning expectations for parenting show that we as father and son still have much to learn about each other. Norman MacLean, expressed it this way when he remembered his father in *A River Runs Through It:*

> It is those we live with and love and should know who elude us. Now nearly all those I loved and did not understand when I was young are dead, but I still reach out to them.[2]

Deanna

My daughter also wrote her story in 1993, when she was sixteen; she is now twenty-one years old. She had an encounter at this time in her life with a high school teacher who expressed discriminatory and unfair disapproval of Deanna as a result of a minor classroom infraction.

The teacher said, "I could expect this kind of behavior from a nonbeliever . . . but you! You're a *Christian!* I am really disappointed, and I'm going to speak to your father."

I don't remember the specifics of Deanna's transgression, but apparently, this verbal lashing was provoked when Deanna stretched the truth regarding class tardiness. The teacher never did follow through with her threat to call me, and my daughter finished the course with a B+ final grade.

When this incident occured, I had just read a startlingly parallel story in Cameron Lee's book, *PK*. Here is the similar event described by Lee:

PK's may find themselves continually reminded of the expectations of sainthood, sometimes expressed in public ways.
William Hulme tells this story:

I know of one parsonage family who were determined these
stereotypes [PK's as little saints] would not affect their children. They talked things over with the congregation, and all
seemed to understand. One day, however, one of the children,
along with others, got into some trouble at school. In repri-
manding the students, the principal [who was not a member of
the congregation] said to their child, "The others I can understand, but you, a minister's child, I don't understand." The
mother was furious when she heard about this. "When it's not
the congregation," she said, "it's the public school. How do
you get away from these pressures?"[3]

The uncanny resemblance of my daughter's story to Lee's
illustration as well as the timing of the encounter left me with a
feeling of awe rather than anger. I became angry later, as did the
mother in the previous quote, but my initial response was wonder.

"How about that!" I mused. "The experiences of PKs *do* take
on some universal qualities." Deanna not only experienced the
shame because of her faith, but because the teacher knew I was a
minister.

This event prompted me to pay closer attention to the effect the
label "minister's daughter" might be having on Deanna's life. She
likely suffers more than what she reveals through her outward
behavior and communication.

Deanna is by nature an easygoing, achievement-oriented person
who appears unaffected by the craziness of people around her. For
instance, if she recapitulates a story in which one of her friends has
behaved badly, Deanna's typical response is as follows: "So and
so will get over it. I can't do anything about her bad mood, so I
don't sweat it."

I have taken my daughter's words at face value and assumed her
demeanor reflected what was really going on inside. For the most
part, I believe she handles life in an easygoing manner. Nevertheless, the outcome of the confrontation with the biology teacher
prompted Deanna to express some strong feelings over the injustice

of the PK label, and she ultimately revealed some deep and angry feelings about our expectations of her as PK parents.

I have found it difficult to hear my daughter vent these feelings. One reason for this is that not only am I the minister, but I am also the father who has the unenviable task of setting limits for a developing adolescent. (I should confess, however, I'm really not such a tragic hero. When the heat is on about the limits, I typically say, "Go ask your mother.") Nonetheless, the boundaries get defined, and in Deanna's case, she reacts to the limits by acting out anger over her role as a PK.

Despite these tensions of our parent-adolescent relationship, there are legitimate issues and feelings which my daughter has expressed and to which I am trying to pay attention.

Out of this milieu of family experience, Deanna has written her story. As her story unfolds, I will cite parallel disclosures from other PKs as collected by Cameron Lee that support the legitimacy of Deanna's views and their similarity to other PKs views.

Cameron Lee, in his writing on PKs, likens the experiences of preachers' kids to actors in a difficult drama. The minister/parent, congregations, and the outside community intentionally or unintentionally attempt to set the stage, write the script, and define the role of the PK. At the same time, the child/adolescent hollers back, "Just a minute! I'm not these things! I see myself in a different role, on a different stage, and with a different script! Quit shoving me into something that is not me! Pay attention, and listen to the 'me' I want to become!"[4]

Here, then, is my daughter's chronicle.

DEANNA'S STORY

Things I Don't Like About Being a Preacher's Kid

Everyone in the church and sometimes even your parents act as if you have to have the same ethical, moral, and religious views that your parents have. If you're not living your life according to your parents' expectations or the church's, then you are looked down upon and not received into the church or family unit with any eagerness or enthusiasm.

I started finding myself doing things to please my parents or people in church, but they were not my convictions.

Parallel Stories from the Book PK

- I'm not sure if this pressure [having to maintain a certain reputation] was silently imposed upon me by my parents or the congregation, or if it was my perception of what I was supposed to do . . . (p. 93)
- The basic rules of life, such as why I shouldn't steal, were carefully explained, and though they didn't make a great deal of sense to me, I didn't feel overwhelmed by them . . . (p. 93)
- Many of the church's rules made no sense to me . . . I became very confused about true guilt and false guilt, between God's commands and people's rules . . . inside I harbored a repressed rebellion, on the outside I was a very dutiful child . . . (p. 93)
- Lots of people think you're a little saint. Some people find out you're not and try to make you into one. (p. 75)
- It's hard to illustrate, but there always seemed to be an underlying pressure to be a saint.[5] (p. 75)

Deanna Continues . . .

Another thing is that my dad doesn't act the same at church as he does at home. When my dad's up there preaching, I can't help but wonder if his preaching is fake and he really believes what he is saying. Maybe it is because I see all of his faults.

A Parallel Story from PK

When your earthly father is your minister, who is the one who's going to teach you about your heavenly father? It's just very, very confusing. You don't know where one ends and the other begins or how to differentiate them.[6]

Deanna Continues . . .

It also seems as if the church comes before the family, and then in the end, the minister takes out his frustration on the family.

Parallel Stories from PK

- All of their time, energy, and money was going into the ministry.
- I felt unimportant because the ministry got preference over me a lot of the time.
- Our lives were shaped around the needs of the church. Having no money because the church needed it, moving to different towns, not being allowed to do things and go places . . . Dad spent a lot of time on the church and didn't have a lot of time for the family.[7]

Deanna Continues . . .

Another thing I hate is that the church and the community expect you to always go to your dad's church and to always go to church. But I personally don't like going to my father's church because he is my dad, and I can't think of him as a minister.

I believe I could never go to him with problems about myself or God because he's my dad, and I don't think he can leave that out and just tell me what God says. I think my dad will automatically put his own opinion and feelings into it.

Parallel Stories from PK

(Note: I could not locate an exact match to the desire my daughter expresses to have a different minister and attend a different church. However, Cameron Lee's accounts of PKs in conflict with their parents on career choices represent close counterparts.)

- I think the biggest issue for me growing up as a PK has been vocation, career choice. As I reflect on it, I chose to be a minister out of a kind of love-hate relationship with the church. In so many ways I hated growing up in a pastor's home. Yet, I felt an inner push to follow in my father's footsteps, to remain in that identity of church leadership. It is only now that I am able to process some of these circumstances and feel as if I am entering a field because I want to do it . . .

• I struggled with the idea of becoming a missionary. I even started college with the intention of going overseas. I felt it was my duty and obligation to be in the ministry. It wasn't until I was out from under the cover of being a PK and attending a church on my own at college that I realized that God had a calling for my life. I didn't have to do anything simply because it was expected.[8]

Here is further commentary on my daughter's feelings of entrapment to congregational expectations and the perception that she really does not have a pastor.

In Chapter 2, Diana expressed similar feelings about lacking a pastor. These sentiments are expressed because of a need to have a minister outside the family unit who is different from a dad or husband. My son also feels the same way and seeks pastoral support from others outside the immediate family. This raises an issue of need that is generally acknowledged for the minister: "The pastor needs a pastor." Similarly, "The pastor's family *also* needs a pastor," and *my* family has said this needs to be someone different from a dad or husband. As revolutionary as the thought may be—What about the pastor's family attending another church? Why not? If the consideration is too radical, at least options need to be made available to the pastor's family for counseling and care administered by others outside the pastor's family unit.

Deanna Continues . . .

I guess the biggest regret I have for being a PK is that I feel my parents would give me more freedom if I was not the daughter of a minister. I believe my parents would give me more freedom to make my own choices. I know right now what I want to do with my life and how I want to live it. I have done considerable praying and thinking over this. If my dad wasn't a preacher and my parents were more understanding, they would respect my decisions, know they have raised me well, and they would trust and love me enough to let me be me.

Parallel Stories from PK

- I think every PK rebels to some extent. You're raised in this pattern, in this category—you're labeled. At some point you have to decide if you're going to be that or somebody else . . .
- I think that most of the time I was expected to be a very "good" kid. If my friends and I got into trouble, it was assumed that I did not lead us into trouble, but instead got dragged into it myself. I was assumed to be a good kid who got into trouble from his friends—*until I was old enough to create my own identity* (italics mine).
- Although people would deny it, there is unconscious pressure from most for the pastor's children to perform close to perfection . . . There is a tendency for children to resent this "perfection mentality" and to overreact by doing worse things than anyone else in the church.[9]

REFLECTION ON MY CHILDREN AND OUR RELATIONSHIP

I attempted to present the previous material candidly. I asked my children to write what they would like to say for this chapter. This task has had its painful moments; nevertheless, both my son and daughter communicated valuable information.

I have thought that a more accurate assessment of the impact of being a PK would happen in an interview conducted ten years from now. Such a future interview would give a perspective of my children as adults and presumably with families of their own. Be that as it may, here are some current observations.

Throughout the childhood and adolescence of our children, Diana and I have been goal-focused, achievement-oriented persons with multiple interests. Our lives have been more than just our children. This is not to say our children are not important, but we have recognized that children are with us for only a short time, and life goes on after they leave home. Consequently, we have both attempted to lead a life in which a balance is struck between the nurturance of our children and the self-actualization we pursue.

Admittedly, I did not always balance the time spent pursuing dreams with adequate nurturance of my children. On the other hand, my wife really gave her life for the children and has only recently taken up career advancement as Deanna and Dan Aaron have become more independent.

All these things considered, how has this life our children have experienced with us affected them and their future happiness and self-fulfillment? Several things come to mind:

1. Despite the weaknesses in our family structure, both of our children lived in a home that nowadays is an anomaly: we are the original parents; we are not a blended family.
2. Our children, despite the parental failures they experienced, appear to have adjusted well to the real world. They are both resourceful, achievement-oriented self-starters. Somehow, the two of them have been able to adjust to the dysfunctions they experienced and have learned to live a life that is meaningful and fulfilling to themselves.
3. Neither of our children are afraid to communicate, and they seek our counsel when circumstances so warrant.

I recently discussed the dynamics of parenting, good or bad, as viewed by the children with a colleague who is a licensed marriage and family counselor. This colleague, who is a woman and fifteen years my senior, offered this insight:

> Dan, every child has to come to terms with parental failures. We do the best we can, but there is just so much of us, and the needs of the children are endless. Nevertheless, they do survive, and as they must, our children have to take responsibility for their lives and make of them what they will, despite their disappointments over us and their perceptions of our failures.[10]

The Meaning of Love

In conclusion, some of the most valuable insights that I have gained in recent years are how my PK children perceive they are loved.

My son equates love with time and attention. When he calls me on the phone or when he wants advice, he perceives that I love him when I give time to listen to his problems and help him with decisions.

Deanna, on the other hand, perceives that what I *do* for her is an act of love. For example, my daughter had a strong desire to establish her independence. On her sixteenth birthday, I found her looking sad and dejected, sitting on the edge of a new daybed we had bought her for a present. When I asked her what was bothering her, she said, "I wanted the keys for my own car more than I wanted this daybed."

I was somewhat taken aback, but I listened. She was expressing that her own car as a rite of passage would be a step toward her dream of becoming an independent, responsible adult. Thus, Deanna was saying, "You will show me that you love me by doing (buying) what I need to achieve greater independence."

Deanna was given the keys to a new Hyundai just after her sixteenth birthday along with a long list of conditions. That made no difference. She was willing to follow the rules and work to help pay the costs. The important thing was that she got the car—and that her dad cared about her dreams too.

The next chapter is concerned with strategies for developing a healthy family model for the minister and his wife and children. First, I give a rationale for marriage and parenting based on the Bible, nature, and human history. Second, I offer suggestions for a healthier home life that will include:

1. developing a more equitable sharing of family roles between the husband and wife, and
2. exploring ways to keep communication within the family open and effective.

SECTION III:
THE PASTOR AND HIS FAMILY

Chapter 5

The Bible, Nature, Human, and Church History: Warnings and Mandates for Family Nurture

Protestant congregations commonly expect the minister to come equipped with a family. The pastor's family (preferably an Ozzie and Harriet type) is considered a necessary appendage.

Unfortunately, such congregations and even some ministers are unable to recognize that the pastor's family is more than a convenient asset. The pastor's family is a social organism of which the minister is only one part. The pastor and his family are as one in this organism.

The problem of viewing the pastor and his role apart from his family centers in expectations that he function in ministry as a bachelor. Either from within the minister or from his congregation, there is a misconception that encourages the pastor to function as a single man with no responsibilities except his immediate personal needs and those of the congregation. The ironic result of such expectations is the estrangement of the minister from his family. Here is how the estrangement occurs.

On the one hand, a church may demand the minister come to his calling with a family as part of the package. On the other hand, the same minister may be expected to serve the church as if his family did not exist. A minister who serves under these expectations will have little time to meet the needs of his family. Consequently, the pastor's family in this circumstance will become mere ornaments of the parish—dusty, neglected, and ignored.

To treat the pastor's family in such a heedless manner causes the whole church to suffer. First, the pastor's family suffers abandonment.

✓ Second, the congregation suffers because the pastor fails to practice what he is expected to preach to his people: "Love one another and care for one another in your families." A connected, interdependent family unit appears to be very important to God, as the following biblical passages illustrate.

BIBLICAL REFERENCES TO THE FAMILY
AND THEIR IMPLICATIONS
FOR THE PASTOR'S FAMILY

Genesis 2 is a primary reference which illustrates that a family is not a collection of individuals who act in isolation. For example, "Then the Lord God said, 'It is not good that man should be alone; I will make a helper fit for him' " (Genesis 2:18, RSV).

When we read further in Genesis, we discover that the dawn of the human family came with the creation of a woman. A man would no longer live alone.

> . . . and the rib which the Lord God had taken from the man he made into a woman and brought her to the man. Then the man said,
>
> "This at last is bone of my bones
>   and flesh of my flesh;
> She shall be called Woman
>   because she was taken out of Man."
>
> Therefore a man leaves his father and his mother and cleaves to his wife, and they become one flesh. (Genesis 2:22-25, RSV)

The origin of the first family came with the uniting of a man with a woman: separate flesh became one flesh. Such words are spoken in wedding vows, but their application goes far beyond mere ritual. Separate flesh united to become one flesh is the life of a married couple. Although the man and woman in a healthy marriage retain individual identities, neither functions alone: two have become one.

Since the pastor and his mate are one flesh, they, as a totality, are the pastoral ministry of a church. This connection has nothing to do with whether the wife chooses to be involved in her husband's church. In fact, the wife may attend another church. Notwithstanding, the pastor and his spouse have become one flesh through marriage vows, and thus, no person or entity has any justification to treat the pastor or his wife as disconnected persons.

Let us take this analogy further. A common practice in some churches is to impose a work and social agenda upon the pastor's wife apart from her husband's schedule. Besides being uncivil, such impositions on a pastor's wife (where personal choice is eliminated) disregard the unity of a pastoral call. The church does not call the pastor and wife separately; the spousal unit has been called. Further, this spousal unit retains the right to determine how the partners will function together. Thus, unquestionably, the job description of the minister should not include a separate and implied agenda for his wife.

To further emphasize the need for the pastor to care for his wife and family, we will consider some New Testament scriptures. The Apostle Paul affirms the oneness of the marital unit in Ephesians 5:28-31:

> In this same way, husbands ought to love their wives as their own bodies. He who loves his wife loves himself. After all, no one ever hated his own body, but feeds and cares for it, just as Christ does the church—for we are members of his body. "For this reason a man will leave his father and mother and be united to his wife, and the two will become one flesh. (NIV)

I would argue further that children produced in this one-flesh union will share the qualities of this unity as long as they are nurtured by the parents and coexist in the family. Here are three reasons to support a union of children with the husband and wife:

1. Children have derived their lives from the substance of both parents.
2. Children change a couple into a family.
3. Children represent the biological purpose of marriage.

THE BIOLOGICAL PURPOSE OF MARRIAGE

The biological/natural purpose for the coming together of a man and woman is procreation. The mating process is the means through which our species is perpetuated. Not all marriages produce children, but the expected biological outcome of mating is procreation.

Brad Darrach asserts that nature's purpose of creation is procreation:

> To nature, individuals are important only as a means of continuing the species. Nature wants individuals to survive long enough to produce offspring and care for them until they in turn can do the same.[1]

Darrach describes our humanity stripped of all else but our capacity to reproduce, which he says is the biological reason for our existence. According to Darrach, once our offspring are able to care for themselves, nature has no further use for us.[2]

Theologically, reproductive determinism is not the sole reason for human existence. We are a spiritual creation as well as a fleshly one. Nevertheless, procreation is a part of God's plan for humankind. William Pinson sees procreation as the purpose in nature for human marriage:

> We are acting as persons created in the image of God when we involve ourselves in responsible procreation. God creates; we procreate . . . through procreation, men and women carry out part of God's plan . . . the continuation of the human race.[3]

This is not to say that every sexual act between a man and woman is meant to produce a child. Part of the purpose of sexual intercourse is to give pleasure and fulfillment to the partners within the covenant of marriage (see Proverbs 5:15-19). However, the fundamental purpose of the sex act is to produce children, and it is this ultimate purpose that creates a family. A couple without children is a couple. A couple that brings forth children becomes a family.[4]

The act of procreation carries a lifetime of responsibility. The man and woman begin life together as lovers. When children are born, the man and woman enter a new dimension: they become parents.

THE RESPONSIBILITY OF PARENTHOOD

According to Dr. Ray S. Anderson, children make a family, and children are crucially placed in the midst of the one-flesh relationship between a man and woman. The mating partners become the mother and father, and these two persons have been given the divine role of humanizing and spiritualizing the child. The child learns humanness and spirituality through the teaching, example, and socialization of the parents.[5]

The Apostle Paul comments on this critical role of humanization and socialization given to parents:

> Children, obey your parents in the Lord for this is right. "Honor your father and mother" (this is the first commandment with promise), that it may be well with you and that you may live long on the earth. Fathers, do not provoke your children to anger, but bring them up in the discipline and instruction of the Lord. (Ephesians 6:1-4, RSV)

William Pinson asserts that a major purpose of the family is to bring stability to society:

> The Bible includes stabilization of society as one of the purposes of marriage. In fact one can hardly imagine a social order without family life. Families form the basis of society; consequently, practically every society has strict laws to protect the family.[6]

Hence, given these views, and the presumption that a minister will at least attempt to represent God's purpose for humanity—the pastor's family should ideally become a model of stability within its social context.

All things considered, how then can a pastor's family model God's purpose for procreation and socialization of children if the pastor does not set aside time to pay attention to his family? And, how can the pastor's family model God's purpose if the pastor's congregation trivializes his family's need for care and health by placing these needs below their own needs?

SAD TALES OF NEGLECT

Tragically, there are many pastors' families that are not healthy, are unstable, and poorly model God's purpose for a family. A primary reason for this sad state of affairs is that too many ministers are not caring for their families.

Could such problems as the PK syndrome, pastor's wife syndrome, and the prominence of divorce among clergy families be ways in which God is trying to get our attention? Is God saying to us, "The neglect of my shepherds' families has gone on long enough! Now is the time to stop missing the mark. These lambs need care!"

Support for this declaration can be found in the introduction to 1 Timothy in the Serendipity Bible. Mari R. Anderson and Judy Johnson address what they identify as the problem of the "straying Ephesian elders." According to Anderson and Johnson, some problems of these straying elders included fouled personal values and an utter failure to manage their family affairs.[7]

Paul addressed this problem of the straying elders by charging Timothy to remind them of their sacred responsibility: ". . . for if a man does not know how to manage his own household, how can he care for God's church?" (1 Timothy 3:5, RSV).

Anderson and Johnson also stated in their commentary that the modern church has failed to recognize the lessons for our time from the unique setting of 1 Timothy. According to the commentators, the issues in 1 Timothy were unique to the Ephesian church. The purpose of the epistle is not to set rules for women and children: the purpose is to correct the straying elders. The straying elders were setting a poor example and were creating severe problems in the Ephesian Christian community:

> First Timothy is not intended to establish church order [i.e., the role of women], but to respond in a very ad hoc way to the Ephesian situation with its straying elders . . .
>
> . . . Paul intended to write his instructions directly to the church but was unable to do so since the local leadership was itself the problem. (Gordon Fee, "The Sticky Wicket" an unpublished paper)[8]

Once again, the fault of the straying elders was their failure to properly manage and care for their families (1 Timothy 3:4-5).

Finally, lest we believe only contemporary ministers have had family problems, Ruth Tucker gently discloses to us that a number of our heroes in church history experienced serious difficulties with spouses and families. The home life of many of these venerated clerics fell woefully short of a model their churchgoers could emulate.[9]

The Pastor's Family: A History of Neglect

Ruth Tucker unmasks the truth of historically dysfunctional clergy families in her book, *Private Lives of Pastor's Wives*. Here are just a couple of the stories.

John Calvin

John Calvin has been remembered as an authoritarian minister, but apparently, he was also a man who was very sensitive to criticism and easily hurt. Further, he was a poor diplomat. His wife, Idelette, not only had to endure community opposition to her husband's ministry, she also had to support Calvin through other emotional struggles. Also, the Calvin family was laid aside and neglected when this clergyman battled through conflicts in his ministry. Calvin's wife died as his stepchildren approached adolescence, and years later, his stepdaughter, Julia, was convicted of adultery.[10]

Samuel Wesley

Samuel Wesley was a clergyman and father of John and Charles Wesley. He was also a man who did not get along well with his parishioners. His wife and children suffered insults from a community that may have reacted more to the minister's personality flaws rather than his piety. Further, Samuel Wesley would not tolerate the differing political viewpoints of his wife, Susanna. This led to the couple's separation. Samuel eventually returned to the family but was soon sent to debtor's prison.

Tucker's story of the Wesley family is a sad tale of a mistreated wife and emotionally abused children. The marital breakdown that occurred in the Wesley household affected the whole family unit. Although the family is remembered for its two famous sons, John and Charles, only ten of nineteen children survived to adulthood.

Despite the mother's best efforts, the Wesley daughters did not grow to meet Susanna's expectations of successful children. Some reasons for the disappointing outcomes may be linked to experiences these daughters had with marital turmoil in the Wesley household. Additionally, the daughters may have been affected by the father's emotionally abusive and patronizing attitude toward women. Here, according to Ruth Tucker, are the tragic stories of five daughters of Samuel and Susanna Wesley:

- Emila lashed out at her father through letters to her brothers. She made a poor marriage choice in her forties and divorced.
- Susanna was described by her mother as wicked. She bore four children and divorced.
- Hetty ran away with a man who falsely promised to marry her. She being with child hastily married another man who was a heavy drinker and treated her cruelly.
- Martha married a minister who ran off with a mistress to the West Indies.
- Only Nancy had a long and happy marriage.[11]

Likewise, further evidence of a multigenerational transfer of family dysfunctionality may have surfaced in the stormy marriage of John Wesley. He and his wife struggled through intense years of conflict, according to one historian.[12]

These stories are only a few of many recounted by Ruth Tucker, who indeed discloses that we cannot find comfort in any "good old days" of pastors' families. Without knowing the psychology or terminology for dysfunction, pastors' families in church history since the time of Luther have endured maladies that we think are unique only to this generation. Here is just a small list of the sufferings of ministers' families in history:

1. Many families have experienced emotional and physical abuse from the pastor.
2. Pastors' wives have suffered through the scandals of alleged minister affairs.
3. Pastors' wives have had to cope with and minister to their husbands' various depressions and psychological problems.
4. Spouses and children have generally endured as second-class citizens in Christian communities that only distantly understood their problems and offered rare comfort.

RESPONSIBILITY FOR CHANGE

Our predecessors have sinned just as we have sinned, but the burden for change falls upon us. We bear the responsibility for change not only because we have history to teach us, but also because we have fresh technology and expanded knowledge. This is *the* generation that has the tools and resources to transform the way the pastor's family is treated.

The unique *pastor's family* that is deserving of greater respect and care in our churches collectively shares these qualities:

1. Members of the pastor's family are human and vulnerable.
2. The family needs the care and attention of its members, which includes the care of the pastor.
3. This family is subject to the same problems and challenges that all families face.
4. The pastor's family may need counseling and professional intervention from outside its own boundaries.
5. This family needs its privacy.
6. This family needs grace and room to grow.
7. The pastor's family will not necessarily have the same spiritual intensity as the pastor, nor will this family have the same spiritual intensity as certain congregational members.
8. At the same time, some members of the pastor's family may have a deeper spirituality than the pastor himself.

9. The pastor's children are the same as all children. PK does not have to be the self-fulfilling prophecy of a stereotyped, insubordinate minister's child whose behavior brings shame to the church and the minister's family.[13]

10. Love from the congregation and community will cover a multitude of sins.

Jesus said, "Everyone to whom much is given, of him much will be required . . ." (Luke 12:48a, RSV). I believe this passage aptly describes the times in which we live. We have been given history, technology, and knowledge. Maybe, through these gifts, we can change the status of the pastor's family within our churches. We can assist in the healing of past wrongs by changing the way this family is treated and consequently bestow upon it a place of honor in our Christian communities that is long overdue.

Chapter 6

Treasures in Family Discontent

Psychologist Arch Hart encouraged ministers in a conference on personal development to value the discontent expressed by family members and particularly the complaints expressed by the pastor's wife. "Bitching gives valuable information," says Dr. Hart.[1]

The seeking of treasures (valuable information) in family complaints and unhappiness has not been one of my favorite pursuits. Discontent disturbs the peace—my peace—and I typically react to this situation by begging to be left alone. When the issues surface, you might find me saying such things as, "Hey! I'm trying my best! . . . I don't have time to deal with this! . . . Have some consideration! Can't you see I am under stress?"

My erroneously perceived entitlements as the male head of the household plus some dynamics in my family of origin may explain part of this defensive reaction to family conflict. First, as with other males (who still hold the sexist view that a man's home is his castle), I see my home as a sanctuary. The world is a jungle that stops at my front door. I dream of my home as a place of peace where I can regroup, retreat, and relax. Consequently, when conflict surfaces inside the home and threatens to be as disruptive as what is going on outside, I react just as Dr. Huxtable often did in *The Cosby Show:* "I don't care! Do what you want! Go ask your mother! All I want is peace!" Hence, you can see that my natural reaction to conflict is to treat it as an intrusion.

A second probable cause for my defensiveness likely relates to my family of origin. I was raised in a household of heavy drinkers. Conflict in such a household is most common when drinking is heavy. Further, the family conflict that is provoked by alcohol is usually unfocused, random, without purpose, and ultimately forgotten by the perpetrator when he/she is sober. Thus, I have experienced family conflict in the past as out-of-control behavior. My reaction to these prior commotions was to avoid, placate, or get things under control. For these reasons, I have not found it easy to think of conflict as a healthy part of family living and growth.

A FRESH LOOK AT FAMILY CONFLICT

Since I have become more aware of some inappropriate expectations for family life as well as some unique issues from my past, I am attempting to understand and manage family conflict with fresh perspectives. Here are some changes I desire to make:

1. Instead of the "Oh no, here comes trouble" defense mode, I have been trying to relax and learn to listen to the complaint. If complaints do offer valuable information that can improve the overall health of family relations, then the appropriate response is to listen carefully.

   Such listening is a standard practice in business. Most companies want customers to submit complaints because they help a business correct problems in order to keep its customers. The same principle applies to the family. If problems are vocalized, they can be addressed and corrected, and thus the family can avoid more serious trouble in the future.
2. I am making a diligent effort to lay aside a "don't bother me again" attitude and focus on the concerns expressed by either my wife or children.
3. I seek to develop viewpoints that embrace conflict as something valuable and not as an out-of-control, alcoholic behavior.
4. I seek to replace a mental outlook which perceives conflict as intrusion with a mental outlook which perceives conflict as valuable.[2]

What Is Valuable About Family Conflict?

Authors Peter Menconi, Richard Peace, and Lyman Coleman view family conflict as inevitable. These writers state:

Even the most loving families experience friction when people live under the same roof. The strains of keeping a marriage healthy, raising children, and making ends meet combine to make a fertile soil for family conflict. [Nevertheless, say the authors] . . . Family conflict doesn't have to blow a family apart . . . conflict can actually draw a family together.[3]

Based on these observations, here then are some possible values of family conflict.

Conflict Provokes Communication

Conflict compels people to talk to one another. There is a problem and this problem has to be fixed. According to William Pinson, communication is a necessary ingredient in healthy family relationships:

Communication is another essential ingredient to good relationships . . . communication must involve words for people to understand each other. Thus, to build relationships, family members must talk with one another, discuss matters of mutual concern, and share dreams and ideas.[4]

Dr. Pinson cautions that communication should not be all negative (conflict oriented). Nevertheless, if problems are developing, and family members are not talking, conflict is one way to get the phones ringing within the family unit.

Conflict Helps Us Become Better Acquainted

I speak from experience on this topic. The reason I know Diana as well as I do is because we have worked through many conflicts in our marriage. Moreover, we will continue to have issues that pressure us to confront, communicate, and solve problems. Nevertheless, we recognize that these conflicts have helped us understand each other and love each other more fully.

Conflict Releases Pent-Up Emotions

Herbert Fensterheim and Jean Baer encourage married couples to engage in conflict because they believe it is good for the relationship:

Verbal conflict between intimates is not only acceptable, especially between husbands and wives; it is constructive and highly desirable. Couples who fight together are couples who stay together—provided they know how to fight properly.[5]

These therapists contend that the expressing of emotions such as anger in an intimate relationship is necessary to develop and maintain closeness. They go on to say that a "public face" may be an asset in certain jobs or uncomplicated social settings, but keeping a "public face" in an intimate setting can't work because it is impossible to communicate or become close to a person if someone is wearing a mask.[6]

One reason many of us may avoid conflict could relate to confusion we have about healthy relationships. For instance, I had a grandmother who prided herself on maintaining a household in which neither she nor anyone else ever said a harsh word to one another. My grandmother strongly believed verbal conflict was bad. Correspondingly, this same grandmother believed that any negative feelings were bad and that the person who had such feelings had no right to them and should thus deny their existence. She really believed in "peace at any price" in order to avoid conflict. Also, when I reflect on my grandmother's behavior, I realize her insistence on suppressing conflict was a way of controlling others in the extended family.

Similarly, we receive confusing subliminal messages about conflict via television. Conflict on television is frequently depicted as a negative and destructive force. People don't get along so they fight and end up killing or maiming one another.

Further, in an ironic contrast to program violence, television advertising frequently paints rosy pictures of happy families riding around in new cars and wearing new clothes with carefree abandon. These television families live a "don't worry, be happy" existence. Moreover, if there is any conflict, television advertising rarely depicts people communicating to solve significant problems. Instead, the problems in advertising revolve around the brand of shampoo you use or the price of the car you buy. The message conveyed is that these things are your real problems. Find the right car, or change your shampoo, and your troubles will be over.

Consequently, because of mixed messages from the media and negative family experiences, many of us are confused and have trouble discovering the good in working through conflict.

Conflict Identifies and Clarifies Problems

As stated in the beginning of this chapter, "bitching," i.e., conflict, is valuable because it clarifies just exactly what problems exist in a relationship and how these problems affect individuals.

When John Bradshaw describes a functional family system, he lists as a first rule that problems are to be acknowledged and resolved. He goes on to say that problems will exist and conflict will be inevitable because in a healthy family each person is unique:

> The rules in a functional family will be overt and clear. Husband and wife will be aware of their family differences in attitudinal, communicational and behavioral rules. These differences will be understood and accepted as neither right nor wrong. . . . Each partner will be working toward compromised solutions. This certainly does not mean there will never be any conflict. *The capacity for conflict is a mark of intimacy and a mark of a healthy family. Good healthy conflict is a kind of contact.*[7] (Italics added)

Given these reasons for the value of conflict in building healthy family relationships, we will now consider some strategies for conflict resolution.

Conflict Resolution

John Bradshaw stresses that dysfunctional families are families in which communication has been cut off or distorted. Dysfunctional families typically have a script created by a dominant family figure or tradition that tells members how to feel. Individuation is not permitted, and feelings must either be denied or controlled.[8]

The counterpart of a dysfunctional family is the free-flowing exchange and open communication that characterize a functional family. Bradshaw lists the five freedoms developed by family therapist Virginia Satir, that promote such healthy communication:

1. The freedom to see and hear [perceive] what is here and now rather than what was, will be, or should be
2. The freedom to think what one thinks, rather than what one should think
3. The freedom to feel what one feels, rather than what one should feel
4. The freedom to want [desire] and to choose what one wants, rather than what one should want
5. The freedom to imagine one's own self-actualization, rather than playing a rigid role or always playing it safe[9]

Through these freedoms, Bradshaw suggests families can develop effective communication.

In consideration of Satir's model, Bradshaw first proposes that we need to have a highly developed awareness of who we are as individuals and how we respond to the external process of others. Second, he challenges us to be active listeners, matching the content of speech with external signals such as body language and tone of voice. For instance, someone who yells "I'm not angry!" with an aggressive stance and a growling voice is communicating an incongruent message. Third, Bradshaw provokes us to address generalizations that mask true feelings or reveal prejudices. Examples he gives include, "You can't trust a woman." "You make me sick." "Baptists are devil worshippers." Bradshaw suggests we confront persons who make such statements, ask them why they spoke in such a way, and ultimately, encourage such persons to reveal their true feelings. Fourth, Bradshaw says we must be willing to disclose what we really feel, want, and know:

Good communication involves good self-awareness. This demands that one have very clear boundaries. One takes responsibility for one's own feelings, perceptions, interpretations, and desires. One expresses these in self-responsible statements using the word "I." Differentiation also means that I don't take responsibility for *your* feelings, perceptions, interpretations, and desires.[10]

HEALTHY COMMUNICATION
AND THE PASTOR'S FAMILY

Where does all this fit into creating healthy relationships in the pastor's family? I see first of all that each member of the pastor's family has the right to feel what he/she wants to feel about the family as it relates to the local church. For example, if the children want their pastor/father to spend more time at home, the children should have the right to express this. Second, members of the pastor's family should have the freedom to express opinions about the local church and its operation without feeling pressured to conform to a prescribed way of thinking. Third, members of the pastor's family should have the freedom to participate in the life of the local church and denomination by personal choice and commitment, and they have the right to make these choices without pressure to conform to demands of individuals outside the family unit.

The exercise of this freedom was recently expressed by my wife in a meeting with a denominational official of our church. The incident involved some implied expectations that had surfaced about my wife's role in the church and denomination. Additionally, there were some assumptions made as to values we were expected to hold about certain programs being presented by the denomination.

A sensitive issue that arose was a demand for my attendance at a conference which would have separated us for ten days. I did not want to attend this conference but chose not to speak up because I didn't want to cause trouble. Diana, however, was outraged at the imposition of forced attendance, and she did speak up. Here is what she said:

> Wait a minute! I want the right to say "no." The conference you are asking my husband to attend is not good for us or our family at this time. We will miss our own vacation. We need time together.

My wife also addressed what she considered to be an irrational and nostalgic veneration of the conference grounds. She pulled no punches when she referred to the place as a "sacred cow" and "idol."

Understandably, the moments were tense as Diana took her liberty to clarify who she was and what her boundaries were. However, over time, this assertive behavior earned Diana respect and offered opportunities for authentic dialogue with the administrator.

MORE FREEDOM FOR THE PASTOR'S FAMILY

Here are some additional insights on the subject of Satir's five freedoms. I have come to realize that neither my wife nor my children have to believe or commit to the same things I do. Virginia Satir's fourth freedom was the freedom to desire and choose what one wants rather than what one is supposed to want. I believe this is the freedom God gives us, as we are not forced into a life of faith (John 8:36; Galatians 5:1).

Further, I recently learned a lesson on acceptance of personal freedom and the uniqueness of a family member. My son and I were in conflict over his plans to quit college and enlist as a firefighter with the U.S. Forest Service. I spoke to my son from my frame of reference and value system. I knew his education would give him more and better options if he stayed in school. Nevertheless, Dan Aaron said, "Dad you've got to let me make my own choices. If I want to fight fires, that is my decision."

Unquestionably, my son is right. He does make his own decisions, and at the same time he takes the responsibility for his decisions just as I do for mine. He is entitled to his freedom. If consequences of his decisions have unfortunate outcomes, and he returns for help, then I can welcome him again just as the father did in Luke 15.[11]

Thus, I am learning to give members of my family the freedom to be themselves. I am attempting to be as open and honest in my communication as possible. Also, I seek to develop a home environment in which all members can develop and maintain boundaries of individuation and the rights to true feelings and desires. I can do nothing less as their pastor.

Edwin Friedman calls this freedom to be ourselves *differentiation*. Friedman defines differentiation as follows:

. . . the capacity of a family member to define his or her own life's goals and values apart from surrounding togetherness pressures, to say "I" when others are demanding "you" and "we."[12]

In summation, the healthy family, and the healthy pastor's family, is composed of members who are free to be themselves and free to communicate honestly with one another and with those who interact with the family unit.

The next chapter begins a section titled, "The Pastor and Personal Recovery." This chapter explores a dark side of my call to ministry and how the past may have affected the way I responded to my present family.

August, 1983—We begin our ministry
at Gualala Baptist Church.

May, 1989—Our sojourn at Gualala Baptist Church.

May, 1989—The Pastor's Family bids farewell
to the Mendocino coast of California.

May 16, 1998—The Pastor's Family and Diana's graduation
from Humboldt State University, Arcata, California.

SECTION IV:
THE PASTOR
AND PERSONAL RECOVERY

Chapter 7

The Pastor and Codependency:
Coming to Terms with the Dark Side
of the Call to Ministry

What are my reasons for entering pastoral ministry? Why do people in general respond to the "call" of this vocation? Typically, the call to ministry has been ideally understood as a supernatural prompting or message from God. One of the biblical models of such a call from God is found in 1 Samuel 3. Samuel is privileged to receive and then speak a message of revelation not only for the priest Eli, but also for the people of Israel. Samuel's distinctive call is expressed in the last verse of Chapter 3 and the first verse of Chapter 4:

> And the Lord appeared again at Shiloh, for the Lord revealed himself to Samuel at Shiloh by the word of the Lord. And the word of Samuel came to all Israel. (1Samuel 3:21-4:1, RSV)

A commentary in the *Oxford Annotated Bible* related to the previous passage states that the "word of Samuel" in 4:1 probably means "reputation." Consequently, "Samuel became known and trusted throughout all the land as a man who spoke for God."[1]

Another model of a call to ministry is found in Isaiah 6. Isaiah has a supernatural vision of the Lord sitting on his throne in the temple surrounded by seraphim. One of the seraphim [heavenly beings] takes a burning coal off the altar. The seraphim touches the mouth of Isaiah with the coal, and his guilt is purged. Then Isaiah hears a commissioning call of God, "Whom shall I send and who will go for us?" Isaiah leaps to the opportunity: "Here am I! Send me" (Isaiah 6:9).

(There are many pastors, myself included, who fantasize their call to ministry is equal to this heroic response of Isaiah.)

Still another model of a ministerial call is Paul's Dasmascus Road experience. Here we find Paul, a militant Jew, on a mission to purge Judaism of men and women belonging to the "Way" (Christianity). As Paul approaches Dasmascus, he meets Jesus in the appearance of a blinding light. As a result, Paul's life and his understanding of God are almost instantly transformed (Acts 9:1-9).

For some in the Christian community, Paul's transformation is considered an ideal call to ministry. More than a few pastors have identified themselves as modern-day Pauls, arrested by God on a spiritual Damascus Road to be turned to a life of service and ministry for the cause of Christ.

Beyond these biblical models, some persons consider the desire to make a difference in the world and the human condition through Christian ministry as evidence of a call. Such persons have a vision of the way life could be for individuals, families, churches, and communities, if the Holy Spirit were given the full freedom to intervene in the affairs of humankind. Pastors such as myself are motivated by the possibility of bringing the hope of a "new heaven and earth" (Revelation 21) to a people and a world ravaged by sin, sorrow, and injustice.

These are idealized examples of a call to ministry. However, there is also a dark side to this "call." Researchers of human behavior document that such things as alcoholism, childhood trauma, and other dysfunctions in a family of origin can create a desire to enter ministry or other helping professions. I have had to come to terms with these realities. They are the dark afflictions that have shaped my personality and worldview.

These dark afflictions that may influence a person to enter ministry may also create a behavior called *codependence,* which itself could predispose a person to enter ministry. Codependence is a term used to describe unhealthy, addictive behaviors in human relationships. Pastors, by nature of their roles (and likely by their family histories), are predisposed to codependent behavior.

Richard Peace, author of the book *Codependency,* offers his reader a "Codependency Quiz" that is designed to assess the presence and influence of codependency in the behavior of the respondent. A surprising indicator of codependent behavior is found in Question 9 of this quiz. The instructions state: "Answer yes or no . . . I am a teacher, health care worker, or counselor."[2] A "yes" answer to this question is a possible indicator of codependency.

Question 9 suggests that employment in a helping vocation is a sign of an unhealthy susceptibility to codependency. This implication is disturbing. Why are so many of us in helping professions such as ministry prone to be codependents? The answer becomes apparent when we look into the meaning and characteristics of codependency.

WHAT IS CODEPENDENCY?

Melody Beattie is considered one of the experts on codependency, and she readily admits that a definition is hard to pin down:

> There are almost as many definitions of codependency as there are experiences that represent it. In desperation [or perhaps enlightenment], some therapists have proclaimed: "Codependency is *anything,* and *everyone* is codependent."[3]

Given the problem of defining codependency, I will present these attempts of various writers to explain the term:

> **Melody Beattie:** A codependent person is one who has let another person's behavior affect him or her, and who is obsessed with controlling that person's behavior.[4]
> **Nancy Groom:** Codependency is a self-focused way of life in which a person blind to his or her true self continually reacts to others being controlled by and seeking to control their behavior, attitudes, and/or opinions, resulting in spiritual sterility, loss of authenticity, and absence of intimacy.[5]
> **Richard Peace:** Codependents are people who nourish others, who serve others, who sacrifice themselves for the sake of others, and who are selfless to the point of harming themselves. . . . They help others in order to feel good about themselves.[6]

Anne Wilson Schaef: The codependent is invariably a Good Person. Co-dependents are devoted to taking care of others . . . many become professional caregivers (nurses, doctors, counselors).[7]

Sharon Wegscheider-Cruse: . . . an addiction to another person or persons and their problems, or to a relationship and its problems.[8]

Anne Wilson Schaef suggests the following list of codependent traits. Ironically, the traits mirror the job description for a pastor that many congregations implicitly or explicitly uphold. Keep in mind that Anne Schaef is describing a pathological relationship.

- Co-dependents frequently have feelings of low self-worth and find meaning in making themselves indispensable to others . . .
- Co-dependents are sufferers—Good Christian Martyrs. Their goodness is directly related to their suffering and the rewards they expect (and receive) because they are willing to sacrifice so much.
- Co-dependents are servers. They are the volunteers, the people who hold society together, who set aside their own physical, emotional and spiritual needs for the sake of others.
- Co-dependents are selfless to the point of hurting themselves. They work and care for others to such an extreme that they develop all kinds of physical and emotional problems.[9]

Although most of these characteristics appear to have merit, Schaef and other experts in the study of codependency concur that the sum total of codependent behavior is an addictive attempt to control the behavior and opinions of people by a pseudosacrifice of self. This overcommitment and overinvolvement in the needs, moods, and problems of others is not altruistic but manipulative.

Nancy Groom describes codependent behavior as an act of self-aggrandizement:

If freedom is essential to love, then attempted control is essentially a failure to love. Codependents compulsively manipulate the significant persons in their lives, sometimes blatantly . . .

sometimes subtly. . . . But the resentment of the one being res-
cued or taken care of testifies to the codependent's lack of love
and the emotional payback he or she seeks through manipulation.
. . . Sometimes the savior mentality—the need to be needed—just
feels good.[10]

The issue at hand is not whether or not we choose to care for
others, but rather, "What is our motive?" Jesus echoes this caution
when he warns the faithful, "Beware of practicing your piety before
men in order to be seen by them . . ." (Matthew 6:1, RSV). Genuine
regard and love for another person becomes codependency when
the motive is to control others through supposed acts of kindness.
This is an occupational hazard of pastoral ministry, especially when
codependency is expressed as overcommitment and manipulation
that may impact a pastor's effectiveness if indeed his/her family of
origin was dysfunctional.

Consider these findings of Sharon Wegscheider-Cruse. First, she
believes codependents are primarily people who have the following
characteristics:

1. Currently involved in a love or marriage relationship with an
   addict
2. Had at least one alcoholic parent or grandparent
3. Grew up in an emotionally repressive family

Second, given the pervasiveness of these problems, Ms. Wegscheider-
Cruse believes codependents make up 96 percent of the population.[11]
Third, Wegschieder-Cruse found 83 percent of all nurses are firstborn
children of alcoholics and consequently are codependents by definition. (I wonder how many ministers are firstborn children of alcoholics.)

Thus, Wegscheider-Cruse contends that codependents arise out
of the dysfunctional family and social systems of which they were a
part, and a symptom of codependency can be the choice to enter a
helping profession.

At this point, I would like to relate a brief history of my family of
origin, which I recognize has influenced (if darkly) my desire to
enter ministry. The influence of my family of origin stands along-

side the supernatural aspects of my call. Correspondingly, I recognize my vulnerability to this family history and my susceptibility to codependency.

MY FAMILY OF ORIGIN

The family of origin into which I was born was a family where heavy drinking was prominent. Both my mother and father drank heavily, yet neither ever admitted that alcohol was a problem in the family. My parents' responses to their alcohol use have been the following: "We're no different than anyone else. . . . Everybody drinks. . . . We have a beer to unwind. . . ."[12] My three brothers also appear to be heavy drinkers. Two deny they have a problem. Only my youngest brother admits his addiction, and he has also stated he will not give up his use of alcohol.

Finally, although I never became a heavy drinker, I reacted to my family's dysfunction in a predictable way. Physicians who study the effects of alcohol on the family speak of the roles children take to cope with alcohol-related behaviors within a family. A daughter may become the family princess; a son may become a family clown; still another son may become a family delinquent to deflect attention from the behaviors of his parents. I know I became a super-responsible overachiever as a result of my reaction to alcohol abuse in my family of origin.[13]

I would like to clarify that my parents were both loving and supportive throughout my childhood. I was well fed and clothed. My parents cared about the welfare and success of me and my brothers. They attended sporting events, helped out with school pageants, and proudly attended life-passage events such as graduations and weddings. Further, my parents functioned responsibly in daily activities: My father was a good provider with an excellent career history; my mother kept a clean and orderly house and faithfully cared for us as children. Nevertheless, both my parents drank regularly and often heavily.

When I reflect on this past, I see my parents as products of a culture and generation in which the use of both alcohol and tobacco were acceptable and fashionable. My parents were married in 1941 and began their family in 1943. Movies of this period, sometimes called film noir, depicted successful and sophisticated persons with long cigarettes and mixed drinks. These Bogarts and Bacalls were the images of people who lived and loved life to the fullest, be it exchanging glances in an elegant nightclub or exchanging passionate kisses in an exotic locale. These old movies mirror life in the 1940s and depict alcohol and tobacco as icons of sophistication. Hence, my parents' drinking and lifestyle were probably no different from the drinking and lifestyles of their peers.

However, regardless of the accepted use of alcohol in the 1940s, the consequences of heavy drinking include the alteration of mood and severe emotional outbursts. As the oldest child in my family of origin, I ached for the day to be set free from the "crazymaking" turmoil that was caused by my parents' heavy drinking. I hated the interactions I was forced to endure as a teenager, when either my mother or father was drunk. I became their wailing wall and the target of all their frustration and unhappiness when they were under the influence of alcohol. As a result of these unpleasant experiences, I vowed I would not subject any other human being to such suffering.

Nevertheless, I need to say I have not done too well with this vow. Both of my children have complained that I can be both irritable and emotionally distant in my relationships with them. I accordingly recognize the danger that I may be perpetuating a multigenerational cycle of negative family dynamics. I also realize that I have the primary responsibility to break this cycle, and I am attempting to do so by keeping in touch with the needs of my family and the effects of my behavior and moods upon them.

Despite some evident failure to provide a stable and loving presence for my wife and children, I still seek as a major life goal to comfort oppressed persons and relieve emotional suffering in others. I further realize that these goals are in part an outcome of growing up in a home where heavy drinking was a predominant lifestyle. I don't want others to suffer the pain I have suffered. I have a mission to relieve this pain when I can. Consequently, I acknowledge that my experiences as the oldest child in an alcohol-affected family influenced my call to ministry, and I also understand that similar influences affect others who have chosen to be helpers in society.

I have had the opportunity to talk to a number of professionals who have careers as helpers. The majority of those whom I interviewed, be they counselors, psychotherapists, or social workers, admit that negative family experiences in childhood influenced their career choices. In concurrence with Wegscheider-Cruse's research, personal suffering and the traumas in dysfunctional family situations appear to influence the choices of some people to enter human service careers. In my case, the choice to be a minister is a cathartic means of making sense of and giving purpose to some of the painful and absurd experiences of the past.

Notable persons in fields of recovery and psychotherapy who describe traumatic pasts as a reason for choosing a helping career tell these stories:

1. John Bradshaw, who wrote *The Family* and *Healing the Shame That Binds You,* confesses in his works that he is an alcoholic in recovery.
2. Abraham Maslow disclosed in a biography of his life that the source of his theory on the "hierarchy of needs" is derived from experiences, almost too horrible to imagine, that he suffered at the hands of his abusive, sadistic mother.
3. Melody Beattie, Nancy Groom, Anne Wilson Schaef, and authors of just about every book I have read on codependency have experienced firsthand the hell of dysfunctional living and have assumed the misguided characteristics of codependency to cope with the persistent pain of a past they can't forget.

Thus, as I reflect on my personal history, I realize I am in good and plentiful company.

THE ARMY OF HELPERS

Did God permit all this family suffering so he could raise up an army of helpers? If there were no home environments of alcoholism and overresponsible, firstborn children of alcoholics, would we lack the doctors, nurses, policemen, social workers, teachers, and ministers we have today? Does our society have to be dysfunctional in order to produce the rescuers who do so much to stabilize the system and provide comfort? This is a question of theodicy to which I don't have a clear answer. I would say, however, that any pastor who denies the effect of personal suffering, personal weaknesses, and his/her family of origin upon the call to ministry is not being truthful to himself/herself.

When I ponder the issues of our vulnerabilities as ministers (codependency being one of these weaknesses), I am reminded that Jesus didn't call superpastors in his time. Peter was called out of abysmal failure (he denied Jesus at the crucifixion) to become a key leader in the emergence of the early church (Matthew 26:75 and John 21: 15-19). Saul of Tarsus, enraged that the followers of the Way were corrupting Judaism, was on the road to Damascus with a mission of death and destruction when Jesus called him (albeit with a blinding light) to become the apostle of the Gentiles (Acts 9). Other apostles sought selfish control and reputation when they asked Jesus who among them was the greatest (Luke 9:46-48). Still another apostle struggled with unbelief (John 20:24-28). Yet, in the midst of all this human failure and weakness, Jesus called forth leaders for the infant church.

In consideration of the human failure in the early church, we come back to the question I proposed earlier: Do the problems of personal suffering, alcoholism, and family dysfunction become necessary dynamics for a person to choose a helping career? A clear answer is elusive. Nevertheless, I understand that the history of my family of origin with its heavy drinking dysfunction contributed to my decision to become a pastor. Consequently, I am attempting to keep in touch with these human elements and to be alert to the danger that my sincere love and care for others can become overresponsible, pathological, codependent behavior.

However, to know we can behave codependently creates a new dilemma: What is the balance between pure acts of service as a minister to others and the pathology of codependent behavior?

FROM CODEPENDENCE TO THE LOVE OF GOD

Nancy Groom attempts to redirect the "antidependence" reaction to codependence by offering a biblical alternative to self-sacrifice as a means of controlling people and environments. Groom argues that there are such things as genuine caring for others and what she calls a "mutual interdependence," which are a part of our call to Christian life and community. In her book *From Bondage to Bonding,* Groom describes in detail how the bonding love of God is different from codependence.

First, she states that healthy Christian relationships are grounded in a complete dependence upon God.[14] Next, she describes mutual interdependence as an alternative to codependence:

> Mutual interdependence occurs when two persons, secure in God's acceptance, mutually give and receive love and forgiveness without demanding approval or conformity to expectations in return, resulting in spirituality, a balanced view of self, and genuine intimacy.[15]

A third suggestion Groom offers is to transform caring as a means of control into caring as a free choice that expresses the love of God. This is the kind of service and responsibility for others that comes out of prayer and dependence upon God for guidance. The choice to love and care is free because it is not hindered by the desire to manipulate, and there are no demands for reciprocal love or control. She describes this as mutual freedom:

> Freedom from codependency [mutual freedom] means we can be and let be, live and let live without trying to manage anyone's business but our own.[16]

Finally, Groom addresses the risk of choosing to love without control. Says Groom, "If I'm going to love, I'm going to be hurt and uncomfortable."[17] What she is stating here is that love which is freely given is at risk of being rejected, and further, we place ourselves at risk if we attempt to love and care for another without the compulsion to control. The risk and the ultimate power that comes from this type of service to others is expressed in the famous "Serenity Prayer."

> God grant me the serenity to accept the things I cannot change,
> the courage to change the things I can,
> and the wisdom to know the difference.[18]

The application of this prayer, as I understand it for my own life and ministry, is simply that I have no power to control the feelings and actions of anyone but myself. Thus, the choices I make in my ministry will have a foundation not in controlling the mood or approval of the congregation, but rather, I will choose freely to serve as I see God directing, and my choices will be a result of prayerful reliance on the leadership of the Holy Spirit.

FREEDOM FROM CODEPENDENCY WITH THE CONGREGATION

When I cut the bonds of codependency, I not only free myself—I free my family, and I liberate my congregation.

I remember the times I have asked myself, "What will the congregation think?" I remember the compromises I have made that negatively affected the well-being of my family in order to placate the moods of parishioners. I remember when I postponed a vacation, refused to buy something, or forced one of our children to go to church (when there was a need for a time-out). I remember when I caved in to parishioner demands because I didn't want to deal with the possible disapproval. I remember when I was afraid to set limits.

All of these behaviors are unhealthy. Consequently, growth for me is learning to step away from these codependent fears and to set differentiated boundaries that will heal not only my relationships to my family but also my relationships to my congregation.

In the next chapter, I explore ways to develop healthy pastor, family, and congregational relationships. The key to good relationships is defining and setting boundaries.

Chapter 8

Setting Boundaries
and Learning to Say "No":
Benchmarks for Healthy Relationships
Between the Pastor, His Family,
and the Congregation

I will hasten to agree that giving advice about setting limits is much easier than implementing the practice. First, people get upset with "noes" and boundaries. Second, the pressure of taking an assertive stand can be very uncomfortable and lonely. The following story should help explain my problem.

A short time ago, the present congregation we serve suggested we set a date to bowl as a church recreational activity. The idea was a good one, and a Sunday afternoon was selected. The day came for the event, and as the small congregation gathered before our service began, one of the women asked my wife if she would be bowling.

Diana politely said, "No, I will not be going, I am going to stay home." Diana set her limits. She realized that on this particular day she needed some rest and personal renewal so she said "no" to bowling.

Despite my wife's gracious reply, you would have thought by the look on this woman's face that my wife had just committed an unpardonable sin. The individual in question was first shocked and then enraged. With murderous looks, she turned away, stormed to her seat, tore open the song book, and spent the remainder of the service staring straight ahead while she talked out of the side of her mouth to her husband. When the service ended, the woman stomped out, and the dark cloud of her anger lingered long after she had left.

I confronted the lady a few days later about the incident, and she said, "Yes, I was very angry and very hurt that your wife did not come and bowl with us."

I took this occasion to explain to the parishioner that my wife's "no" was not a personal rejection directed toward her. Further, I encouraged the woman to allow others to set their own limits while at the same time she should seek to emotionally disentangle herself from someone else's choices.

The substance of this controversy seems fairly trivial on the surface. Nonetheless, church splits have occurred over much less. The infamous and apocryphal church war fought over the color of the sanctuary carpet is just one example of the upset created by people who can't agree and won't accept boundaries.

The point of it all is simply this: to give someone else advice on how to be assertive is far different from being assertive yourself. The heat of someone else's displeasure can be unbearable.

"NO" CREATES UPSET

One reason "no" creates upset is that "no" and other limits restrict the power someone else has over an individual. When a person is told "no," such a person is being asked to respect the time and space of someone else. Understandably, not everyone responds appropriately to such requests because to do so would mean to relinquish power.

According to Anne Wilson Schaef and Diane Fassel, the lust for power and the clamor for control are pathological symptoms of our addictive society:

> . . . the addictive system harbors the belief that it is possible to control everything; in fact the illusion of control begins with the addict's attempt to control self with a substance or a process . . . From this first illusion of control, they believe they can then control what others are feeling as well. Whenever a system is operating out of an illusion of control, it is an addictive system by definition.[1]

If Sharon Wegscheider-Cruse is right, and 96 percent of our society functions addictively, then setting personal boundaries and functioning assertively is not going to be easy.[2]

The second problem which is created by boundaries and "no" is that some individuals interpret these limits as a personal rejection. Thus, "no" creates hurt feelings and ruffled feathers for the overly sensitive.

Third, the role of a pastor carries an expectation of availability, as I have discussed earlier. Nevertheless, guidelines which clarify that there are limits to the pastor's availability create tension in some congregations. The challenge for me is to learn to become comfortable with these tensions and with assertive behavior.

SETTING BOUNDARIES MEANS BECOMING COMFORTABLE WITH ASSERTIVE BEHAVIOR

Peter Wagner, when describing the pastor-as-chaplain role expectation, addresses the stereotypical image of a minister that depicts the clergyperson as a superresponsible, superdiplomatic human being who is the be-all and end-all for every crisis his congregation might experience.[3] The pastor-as-chaplain ideal is very pervasive in today's Christian community. A possible reason for the ascription may be the demoralizing treatment many people experience in society outside the church. Because of negative experiences in the secular world, individuals seek out someone who won't hurt them and who will comfort them through trial and tribulation. This comfort is sought from a compassionate minister with broad shoulders and unlimited time. The pastor-as-chaplain can become a teddy bear on call.

What do people get from teddy bears? Teddy bears are something to hold when you have had a bad day. Teddy bears are soft and cuddly; they provide an abundance of "warm fuzzies." Teddy bears don't cause pain, and they don't set limits.

Granted, there is a nurturing and comforting component to pastoral ministry. At the same time, a minister may also be called upon to exhort, correct, and make difficult decisions. Thus, we have a problem (in a parody of an apocryphal saying attributed to Abraham Lincoln):

You can be a teddy bear to some of the people all of the time, or you can be a teddy bear to all of the people some of the time . . . but you can't be a teddy bear to all of the people all of the time.

Here, then, is the locus of tension. When a minister cannot be or refuses to be the teddy bear, such a minister will discover plenty of persons in his congregation who will be unable to accept him as a prophet or confronter.

If the teddy bear fixation appears incredible, consider these stories about pastor-heroes that are part of the folklore and myth of the contemporary American church:

- "I love my pastor; I can call him and talk to him any time I want, day or night. He will always stop to listen."
- "I love my pastor! When Aunt Matilda got sick, he came to the hospital every day and sat by her bedside until she went home to heaven."
- "I love my pastor. He never has a harsh word to say to anyone."
- "My pastor never puts his needs first. He always thinks of others before he thinks of himself."
- "My pastor never loses his temper."

These preconceptions may be wrong, but what is one to do? Reeducation is one route, but that is not going to keep people from getting upset if a minister refuses to play the roles described here.

I have taken great care to educate my parishioners on assertive behavior, freedom to choose, and religious liberty. I have explained that this is the way I intend to relate to them as well. Nevertheless, despite the nodding heads in church and Sunday school, the sparks still fly when I make assertive choices that conflict with the perennial stereotype of clergy self-sacrifice.

Dr. Robert Schuller acknowledges the ubiquity of the "man/woman of all comfort" pastoral stereotype. Consequently, he strongly believes that the pastor can't play "the heavy" in church relationships; the pastor has to get someone else to do that job for him:

Generally speaking—and it would be a rare exception when this principle would not hold—the pastor should never confront the negative-thinking, obstructionist layman. Another layman should do the confronting and spare the pastor—not for the selfish reason that a pastor is unwilling to suffer the scars of battle, but for the sake of the church.[4]

Nonetheless, a pastor will destroy himself and his family if he doesn't set boundaries, learn to say no, and refuse to be overextended.

Getting Comfortable with Boundaries

Setting boundaries and learning to say no are positive attributes of assertive behavior. Robert E. Alberti and Michael Emmons offer this working definition:

> Assertive behavior promotes equality in human relationships, enabling us to act in our own best interests, to stand up for ourselves without undue anxiety, to express honest feelings comfortably, to exercise personal rights without denying the rights of others.[5]

Alberti and Emmons offer a rationale for assertive behavior that is hard to dispute. The setting of boundaries (including the minister's) promotes healthy human relationships. If the minister refuses to acknowledge his/her need for boundaries, he/she becomes a harried codependent, and the prognosis for this condition is physical and spiritual burnout.

Thus, getting comfortable with self-determined boundaries, means learning to say, "It is all right to take care of myself." The bromide, "If I don't take care of myself, I won't be around for you," conveys the truth of the situation. A burned-out pastor loses his/her effectiveness and power to serve.

In addition, the decision to set limits also means getting comfortable with criticism. The minister who contradicts the preconceptions about unlimited availability needs to become comfortable with the criticism that will follow. Comfort in the face of this criticism is possible if the minister believes he/she is doing right to care for himself/herself. When the minister reaches this state of mind, such a person will stand before his/her accusers with what Edwin Friedman calls a "nonanxious" presence. Here is Friedman's definition and description of this term:

> What Bowen [Murray Bowen of Georgetown Medical School] has hypothesized is a scale of differentiation. Differentiation means the capacity of a family [institutional] member to define his or her own life's goals and values apart from surrounding togetherness pressures, to say "I" when others are demanding "you" and "we." It includes the capacity to maintain a [relatively] *nonanxious presence* in the midst of anxious systems, to take responsibility for one's own destiny and emotional being. . . . Differentiation means the capacity to be an "I" while remaining connected.[6] (Italics added)

Moreover, the effectiveness of a nonanxious presence on limit setting is discussed by educational psychologist Fred Jones. His purpose is to offer teachers some strategies for effective classroom management. These principles, however, apply to more than just education:

> The basic irony of meaning business . . . can be summarized in two statements: Calm is strength. Upset is weakness. When you are calm, who is in control of your mind and body? You are, obviously. When you are upset, who is in control of your mind and body? The person who is upsetting you, of course.[7]

Fred Jones's "calm is strength," as illustrated, parallels Friedman's concept of "nonanxious presence." Jones goes on to offer specific exercises for developing calmness. He suggests that relaxation in the midst of provocation is more a skill than an act of the will. This skill, Jones asserts, can be developed with practice of certain exercises. Some of these include finding a place of solitude before the teaching day begins and learning how to relax through breathing. These techniques, he said, combat the natural fight-or-flight responses of the body.

One of the most useful cues for self-relaxation is a *relaxing breath*. . . . A relaxing breath is an ordinary breath—a slow, shallow breath that fills one-third to one-half of your lungs . . .

The relaxing breath does two jobs: (1) it calms your mind and body, and (2) it slows you down and paces you so that your movements are unhurried. . . . With training it triggers a learned "let down" reflex which counters the mobilization of fight-flight.[8]

Fred Jones offers these exercises as a means of developing calm in contentious settings. The disciplines of prayer and meditation appear to be complementary exercises to Jones's suggestions on how to become comfortable with boundaries. Jones, as a secular author, apparently understands the necessity of inner quiet as a key to effectiveness.

The psalmist, however, predates such a discovery, with the prompting of inner quiet as a spiritual discipline.

> O Lord, my heart is not lifted up,
> my eyes are not raised too high;
>
> I do not occupy myself with things
> too great and too marvelous for me.
>
> But I have calmed and quieted my soul,
> like a child quieted at its mother's breast;
> like a child that is quieted is my soul.
>
> O Israel, hope in the Lord
> from this time forth and for evermore. (Psalm 131, RSV)

Self-Talk

Besides the need to exercise physically and spiritually to develop a "nonanxious presence," the minister can also learn to get comfortable with boundaries through *self-talk*.

Randolph Sanders and H. Newton Malony identify self-talk as silent messages or cognitions through which we process situations we encounter. The authors believe that negative self-talk hinders individuals from acting assertively and speaking up about personal limits.[9]

Sanders and Malony believe that *creative self-talk* can counteract negative cognitions about limit setting. They suggest that creative self-talk (while recognizing the therapy has both pros and cons) addresses an interpersonal situation with the purpose of solving a problem. "Negative self-talk," the writers contend, "has no such purpose."[10]

The authors then provide examples of the differences between negative and creative self-talk, for example:

Negative Self-Talk	Creative Self-Talk
"They'll think badly of me if I speak up."	"I am valuable as a person because God says so, not because of what others think."
"Since I am a Christian, I have no right to say anything."	"Being a Christian may or may not mean that I speak up."
"Jesus said, 'Love your neighbor as yourself,' and that means I should forget my own needs."	"Jesus said, 'Love your neighbor as yourself,' and that means I accept my love for myself and use that to help me love others more."[11]

LIMIT SETTING AND SCRIPTURE

I, along with other clergy, struggle with the last two examples of negative self-talk because they are taunts that appear to reenforce in a biblical manner that Christians and especially ministers shouldn't speak up for themselves. Further, as I described in the opening of this chapter, we encounter abundant numbers of our congregation who firmly believe self-effacement is a prime virtue of pastoral ministry. Thus, part of my problem is becoming comfortable with the idea that the image of the self-effacing pastor is an incorrect value which needs to be changed within a congregation.

Sanders and Malony contend that Jesus, who was the divine expression of a pastor, "was confronting, openly angry, and positively assertive toward others."[12] The writers cited as one example Mark 3:1-5. In this passage, Jesus healed a man with a paralyzed hand despite inevitable criticism by some people who accused him of wrongdoing by breaking the Sabbath with this deed.[13] Sanders and Malony noted these examples of assertive action:

> First, Jesus went to the synagogue of his own volition and healed the man despite the fact his opponents were obviously watching him. Second, he explained his behavior to his enemies. Finally, the scripture indicates that Jesus' attitude during the incident was a mixture of controlled anger and sadness. Jesus' words, feelings and behavior were all assertively expressed![14]

Sanders and Malony also argue that the image of Jesus as someone who is nonassertive has actually been created by popular media. Movies and television frequently picture Jesus as someone who speaks in imperceptible whispers with soft music playing in the background.[15] Although soft music and whispers are not real life, nonetheless, they persist in the contemporary mythology regarding the behavior of Jesus and his followers. Such images are very difficult to dispel.

HOW I AM SETTING LIMITS

Despite all the struggles, I am determined to set boundaries and to say "no" through the implementation of the strategies just discussed. Here are some things I am doing.

Family Boundaries

I have discussed with my wife and children their wishes as to their relationship and involvement in our church. Both my wife and children have stated what they want and don't want to do, and they have also expressed the limits of their involvement. I accept these wishes and have communicated them to our parishioners.

My wife is at a stage in her life where she desires to focus on the development of her personal career as an RN and hospital administrator. Her decisions for church involvement are subordinate to the demands of her profession. I accept these choices as valid, and I respect my wife's boundaries in this regard.

Diana and I have two adult children. Our practice with our children, as they have grown into adolescence and adulthood, has been to respect the boundaries they seek to develop. Neither child has been forced to attend my church, and further, we have not forced them to attend any church. There are reasons why I believe these choices have been correct.

First, as I have watched my oldest son grow from adolescence to adulthood, I have seen him embrace a spirituality and relationship with Christ that is not only authentic but theologically sound. My son did so without our interference during his adolescent years. We respected his boundaries and gave him the freedom to encounter God on his own.

Second, when my daughter was in high school, she stated that she had a problem accepting me both as her dad and as her pastor. She perceived the roles as conflicting. She rightly questioned, "How can I talk to you as a pastor about family problems when you are my dad?"

My response was, "Deanna, you are absolutely right. You need to seek out a setting where your needs for pastoral care can be more suitably met."

I have yet to see the ultimate outcome of this respect for my daughter's boundaries. Nevertheless, I do note that she has a deep spiritual hunger that is expressed not only in her prayer life, but also in her desire to read and study the Bible.

Thus, the first step in establishing boundaries between our family and the congregation was to determine my family's wishes and respect those wishes as their boundaries.

Personal Boundaries

Edwin H. Friedman believes the key to effective leadership is to develop what he calls self-differentiation. He describes self-differentiation as follows:

The basic concept of leadership through self-differentiation is this: If a leader will take primary responsibility for his or her own position as "head" and work to define his or her own goals and self, while staying in touch with the rest of the organism, there is more than a reasonable chance that the body will follow.[16]

Friedman also describes three distinctive characteristics of self-differentiated leadership. The first is that the leader must stay in touch with his followers. The second is the "capacity and willingness of the leader to take nonreactive, clearly conceived, and clearly defined positions." The third is the capacity to deal with sabotage of the body and the pressure the body will put upon the head to back down from differentiation.[17]

I am attempting to apply Friedman's principles by following a cardinal rule of recovery from codependency: "The only behavior we can control is our own."[18] First, I have determined what my limits are as to the time I need for rest, recreation, and renewal. I am learning to take time out without guilt. Second, I have determined what my personal goals are for my present pastoral call.

Since I am a church planter starting a new church, I am in an environment that is friendly to self-differentiation. There are few sacred cows in a new church so the pastor has more freedom to establish boundaries unfettered by the past. As a consequence, I have been able to establish early on my freedom to choose how I will spend time and employ my gifts. Specifically, I realize one of my stronger gifts is teaching, and another is offering support in small group settings. Thus, I have patterned my ministry around these strengths.

Further, I have recognized that I can't do all things as a founder in this emerging church so I have chosen to wait to implement certain projects or ministries until I can delegate them to someone who has been given the gifts to meet these needs. Hence, the focus I have is to manage my own talents and set limits. At the same time, I keep alert to the dreams of others and consequently give such persons the opportunity to develop ministries that complement their unique gifts.

THE PROBLEM OF "NO"

When it comes to saying "no," I still struggle; I do not like the upset that is generated by saying "no." Nevertheless, I am attempting to be more courageous and to develop strategies that will make "no" more gracious to the receiver. Here are some techniques I employ, some of which express a humorous insight into the idiosyncrasies of human behavior.

First, I use my calendar as a way of saying "no":

"I'm sorry, but that date conflicts with another appointment."

Second, I will appeal to higher authority:

"There are legal restrictions on that type of counseling."

"I have to follow denominational guidelines."

"I am going to have to consult with my wife."

Third, I decline by using personal boundaries as a reason for saying "no" rather than a personal rejection of the requester:

"Thank you for the offer, but I need time for some rest."

"That was very kind of you to ask, but what you want me to do does not fit my personal goals at this time."

"Your suggestion is an excellent one, but I do not see that activity as suited to my spiritual gifts. Possibly there is someone else who has such a gift."

Fourth, another choice is to have someone else say no for you. Generally, my wife acts as this kind of buffer, while in a larger church a secretary would assist in guarding the minister's time and priorities.

Fifth, despite the controversy generated by this technique, I sometimes use an answering machine to screen phone calls. Many pastors have realized that few crisis calls demand immediate action.[19] Therefore, the answering machine has the ability to deflect the "tyranny of the urgent" and at the same time allows me to carefully consider a response to a caller.

In summary, despite all of these good ideas, there is no guarantee that someone won't get upset and angry if I say "no." I have found this to be true, and I have also found that I still compromise myself on occasion by saying "yes" simply because I don't want to deal with the anger of another person. This is also a choice. Sometimes it's appropriate to forestall such anger, but in the long run, I realize running from confrontation is neither healthy for the pastor nor his congregation. Friedman puts it this way:

> Will leadership through self-differentiation always work? Of course not. . . . But the real question is what does it mean "to work"? Effective family leadership is not simply a matter of leading people to a goal or to feeling good about their togetherness. *It must also be judged by criteria such as the growth of the followers and the long-term survival of the family [church] itself.*[20] (Italics added)

Finally, I recognize that boundaries change over time for myself and for my family. As we, the church, and our environment constantly undergo change, personal boundaries and our relationships with one another need to be reassessed. I have made it my personal goal to keep in touch with these changes and thus rewrite the limits as time and circumstance demand. The well-being and spiritual health of all concerned is the purpose for setting these limits and learning to say "no."

Chapter 9 explores the phenomenon of life experiences in the family as a laboratory that develops spiritual maturity and effectiveness in pastoral ministry.

SECTION V:
THE PASTOR AND GROWTH

Chapter 9

The Minister's Family Life:
A Laboratory of Valuable Experience

Naive idealism is one of my weaknesses. I dream of life the way it is supposed to be or the way I want it to be—and like all idealists, I keep bumping into the real world. Some places where I keep bumping into the *real* world instead of the idealized world are the unpredictable turmoils in pastoral ministry. These real-life experiences have forced me to discard a romantic and unrealistic outlook of the pastor and ministry. I don't know exactly where I accumulated all the myths of ministry, but here are just a few that have been abandoned.

First, I have often daydreamed that the ideal pastor is a sort of spiritual Superman or Indiana Jones. This daydream concocts fanciful notions of a superpastor who flirts with danger and disaster but never gets hurt. This nimble hero deftly outruns, outfoxes, or outdances the painful encounters with the real world that most people experience. My conception of this quixotic superpastor has been a strange mix of Jesus, Mother Teresa, Clint Eastwood, Kathryn Kuhlman, Superman, and Billy Graham. This fabricated superpastor becomes a larger-than-life hero who always has the right word, melts the hearts of multitudes, wins the battle over evil, saves everyone, and floats through life unharmed. Finally, when the superpastor saves the day for everyone and makes the world good again, he rides off into the sunset while cheered by throngs of the faithful.

As foolishly as Don Quixote, I have dallied with these dreams. Notwithstanding, I have come to discover that my Rosinante is also a beat-up old horse, my squire is definitely out to lunch, and more than once I have taken a wild ride on the sail of a windmill. The real world is a world of suffering, stress, failures, disappointments, losses, and readjustments.

This world is what parish people experience. Hence, they need pastors who have experienced and confessed to being a part of real life. Pastors who live in cloistered and insulated castles and don't share the suffering of their congregations have little to offer to those who need comfort and support.

Consequently, I am not only learning to see the real world, but also to pay attention to my family in a fresh way. The disasters, stresses, conflicts, emergencies, traumas, depressions, and adjustments that have been a part of our experiences as a family have not been intrusions which I need to get out of the way. All of these tribulations are the substance of life that my congregation experiences too. Accordingly, my family life is a laboratory of experiences from which I draw identity and wisdom to provide my congregation with comfort and support.

From the crucible of the real world, I become one who has shared suffering. I am not aloof. I have struggled, failed, and sought recovery. I meet my congregation on the same plane. We are fellow human beings who need the mercy and grace of God.

BIBLICAL PERSPECTIVES

Suffering has never been one of my favorite words, but it is one of those experiences that all humans share to one degree or another. Further, the Bible appears to emphasize that our own suffering brings us spiritual growth and empowerment to help others.

Jesus Christ As a Model

Recall the archetype of the suffering servant in Isaiah 53, 1 Peter 2:21-24 equates this suffering with the ministry of Christ and then extends the invitation to follow in Christ's steps.

> To this you were called, because Christ suffered for you, leaving you an example, that you should follow in his steps.

> "He committed no sin,
>   and no deceit was found in his mouth."

When they hurled insults at him, he did not retaliate; when he suffered, he made no threats. Instead he entrusted himself to him who judges justly. He himself bore our sins in his body on the tree, so we might die to sins and live for righteousness; by his wounds you have been healed. (NIV)

The Apostle Paul expands on the concept of Christ's suffering and asserts that humility and humanness are the qualities we as Christ's followers should emulate.

Do nothing out of selfish ambition or vain conceit, but in humility consider others better than yourselves. Each of you should look not only to your own interests, but also to the interests of others.
Your attitude should be the same as that of Christ Jesus:
Who being in the very nature of God,
did not consider equality with God something
to be grasped,
but made himself nothing,
taking the very nature of a servant,
being made in human likeness,
And being found in appearance as a man,
he humbled himself
and became obedient to death—
even death on a cross!
(Philippians 2:3-8, NIV)

Thus, the model that these scriptures present of the highest qualities of Christ's ministry does not place transcendence first. Instead, the model emphasizes the humble, suffering servant. Philippians 2 also says the preeminence of Christ is an outcome of His willingness to lay aside glory and become human (2:9-11).

The Pastor As a Suffering Servant

As I understand these scriptures, the biblical model of the super-pastor is not a superman but a suffering servant. This is the first role to which we have been called as pastors. Keeping this model in mind, the real world of the suffering servant is far different from my idealized fantasies. Servants clean up messes; they bear burdens; they don't hold seats of honor; they suffer; they support; they care and nurture.

I have also discovered that the pastor who has experienced suffering and who is willing to serve his congregation from the insight gained from these experiences usually holds a better audience with his parishioners. This brings us to some other biblical principles on the efficacy of being human and sharing in the suffering of others.

2 Corinthians 1:3-4 counsels that the ability to comfort someone else in trouble comes from the comfort we receive from God in the midst of our own suffering and troubles:

> Praise be to God and Father of our Lord, Jesus Christ, the Father of compassion and the God of all comfort, who comforts us in our troubles, so that we can comfort those in any trouble with the comfort we ourselves have received from God. For just as the sufferings of Christ flow over into our lives, so also through Christ our comfort overflows. (NIV)

Moreover, 1 Peter 5:10 declares that the innate qualities of spiritual strength and steadfastness (the essence of quality ministry) come through the sufferings we endure:

> And the God of all grace, who called you to his eternal glory in Christ, after you have suffered a little while, will himself restore you and make you strong, firm and steadfast. (NIV)

Finally, the supposed intrusions of family conflicts and troubles are actually my friends, according to James 1:2-5. Instead of viewing these distresses as interruptions, I should view these trials as occasions for joy:

> Consider it pure joy, my brothers, whenever you face trials of many kinds, because you know that the testing of your faith develops perseverance. Perseverance must finish its work so that you may be mature and complete, not lacking anything. (NIV)

I am not going to tell you that I have reached a stage where I throw a praise party for God when the heat turns up and I suffer times of distress. Nonetheless, I at least know the scriptures, and I have developed an appreciation for the past troubles we as a family have survived, and my ability to assist my congregation with their own problems has been enhanced by the experience I've gained in coping with mine.

HOW MY FAMILY HAS BEEN A LABORATORY FOR PERSONAL/PASTORAL GROWTH

Health and Hormones

One of the major crises Diana and I faced was her battle with physical problems related to imbalanced hormones. The problem is understood today as PMS (premenstrual syndrome). Despite the fact that PMS has been the subject of cultural humor and a staple of TV comedy routines, it is no joke. A woman who experiences this hormonal imbalance suffers miserably. I did not understand PMS, and my wife sought almost in vain to find a doctor who would recognize the syndrome and offer therapy.

Notwithstanding, those women who have experienced PMS, and those husbands who have wives who have suffered through PMS, comprehend the stress and pain this problem introduces into the marital relationship.

Diana is an RN, so she is familiar with the history and problems of medical diagnosis. In light of this understanding, she commented recently on the plight of women in earlier generations who were routinely placed in insane asylums when for no apparent reason they became emotionally unbalanced. *The story of Mary Todd Lincoln* is an example.[1]

Diana observes, "I would not be surprised to discover that those supposed 'insane' women actually suffered from PMS or menopause. No one understood those problems in earlier days, and the conditions are still not understood today."

PMS was a crisis in our marriage, primarily because I as a male was too dense to understand what was happening to my wife. The intense conflicts and emotions related to this phenomenon taught me some valuable lessons as a husband and male minister:

1. I have learned to appreciate more fully the sufferings a woman must endure in her physical body.
2. Hormones affect behavior, and a wise pastor will inquire about a person's physical well-being before addressing an emotional or interpersonal problem.
3. There is much that even medical science does not yet fully understand about the human body's effect on mood and behavior. My wife's experience with PMS has opened my eyes to this bigger picture.
4. There is a bromide that admonishes one person to refrain from judging another until one has walked in that person's shoes. Because of my heightened awareness of health, hormones, and the effects on human behavior, I am learning to be "swift to hear, slow to speak, and slow to anger" (James 1:19).

Death in the Family

My father died in the summer of 1990, and this was a very stressful experience for me. His death came on top of other crises, not the least of which was the personal loss of a business which I will discuss in Chapter 11. I viewed my father's death as an intrusion for many reasons.

First, I have long resented having to go through the grieving process connected with the death of a loved one. The likely reason for this struggle is the deep sorrow I experienced when I lost my grandfather at the age of nine. I was very close to my grandfather, and when he died, I experienced an agonizing period of grief. Consequently, at this young age, I resolved never to allow myself to experience such pain again. I was determined to somehow distance myself from relationships that would cause deep pain in the event of death or loss. This resolution as a young child to straight-arm grief and death has persisted into my adult years. The purpose of this has been to provide a buffer and to numb emotional pain.

Nevertheless, when I reflect as an adult on this childhood resolution, I perceive the need to grieve as a part of a healthy healing process to recover from loss. Further, I understand the need to receive supportive intervention to facilitate this grieving process. Armed with this knowledge, I attempted to handle my father's death with good, healthy grief and adequate support. Nonetheless, old reactions and past pain lay just below the surface of present events, and when my father died, I remember thinking, "I do not need this now, and besides that, I really resent the intrusion his death has made into my life."

Hence, my father's death opened a Pandora's box of unpleasant experiences over which I had little control. Further, his death forced me to deal with some issues of my emotional health and spiritual development that I preferred to let lie as sleeping dogs. What have been the outcomes of this sorrowful, unpleasant interlude?

Most important, I have discovered that when I tell my story and share feelings with peers and others whom I can trust my suffering is not unique or isolated. I find that almost everyone has some sadness or family issue that parallels mine. These experiences have universal qualities. Also, because of the death of my father and the coping with family crises that followed, I have become better equipped to support and comfort my parishioners. Members of my congregation have their own tales of death in the family and other crises. The sufferings of our common experiences have become the meeting ground for mutual encouragement and spiritual growth.

Children

Similar to the experience of other parents, I have sometimes felt that the stress of raising my children has been unbearable. The over-arching concern for their physical well-being has probably been the most substantial burden I have carried. Nevertheless, coupled with my concern for their food, shelter, and physical health, I have been one of those parents who has wanted to protect my children from sorrow and tribulation. My irrational pleadings with God have been, "God it's OK if I hurt, but please spare my children."

I suppose I have foolishly prayed my prayer by assuming that all that happens in this world is under the direct control of God and that somehow, if I pray hard enough, God will magically insulate my children from life's uncertainties.

What I understand now is that the world in which my children exist is a mix of God's presence, the influence of evil, and the uncertainties of human free will. 3 John 11 says this: ". . . Anyone who does what is good is from God. Anyone who does what is evil has not seen God" (NIV). In a similar manner, Paul speaks of spiritual warfare in which we all must take part (Ephesians 6:10-20).

Finally, Jesus declared that evil resides in the hearts of men, and it is out of men's hearts that defilement comes (Matthew 15:10-11).

Thus, considering these scriptures, I cannot pray that my children will not experience the real world. Instead of insulating my children from life, *The Lord's Prayer* petitions me "to deliver them from the evil one" (Matthew 6:13, NIV). In addition, I can also challenge them to keep themselves unstained by the world (James 1:27). This does not mean, however, that I can prevent my children from experiencing life, which by its very nature is a mix of good and bad—and a mix of circumstances that are not under my control or my children's.

Knowing this does not make it any easier to cope with the skinned knees, the crises in friendships, the embarrassments, the disappointments, the injustices, the hurts, the unkindness of people, the fights at school, the lack of money to fund that special trip or that school jacket, the trouble with boyfriends, the trouble with girlfriends—trouble in general. In the real world, the kids come home; they hurt; they cry out, and they say things like this: "How come, Dad!" "You made me!" "How come you can't fix my problem, alleviate my pain, pay for my trip, make that person quit hating me, chase away my boredom, help me with that awful teacher . . . make my day?!"

How I wish I could fix those problems! Children know how to create pressure and play our chords of guilt and responsibility. Concurrently, I hate to see them suffer. I want them to be happy all the time. I dream of playing God and magically zapping away their tribulations. Nonetheless, my children tell me later, "Dad, it was good I went through that troublesome time. Trouble has made me a stronger person."

My congregation has children too. What I have gone through with my children, they have also experienced, although sometimes far more intensely. At the same time, since I have suffered as a parent, other parents can freely come and share their deepest hurts and dreams. I will understand, and I will pray for them with conviction and feeling. I am their suffering servant.

SECTION VI:
THE PASTOR
AND SPIRITUAL FORMATION

Chapter 10

Spiritual Formation:
Giving and Receiving Prayer

PROLOGUE

This final chapter of *The Pastor's Family* is really a story of the integration of all that has come before. This integration represents the purpose of why we were given life in the first place. My sufferings, struggles, and life experiences as a pastor have not been random events in a world of chaos and disorder. There is more to the story.

The Apostle Paul's writing is shrouded in mystery in Romans 8, and *predestination* is a difficult subject. Nevertheless, when I read verses 28 and 29 of Romans 8, I perceive that all the battles, choices, and turmoil of our life events somehow (both the good and the bad) come together when we turn to God. Paul says:

> And we know that in all things God works for the good of those who love him, who have been called according to his purpose. For those God foreknew he also predestined to be conformed to the likeness of his Son, that he might be the firstborn among many brothers. (Romans 8:28-29, NIV)[1]

The grand plan of God that Paul describes is the essence of spiritual formation—those *(you, me, . . . we)* who love him and have been called according to his purpose were called (predestined) to *be conformed to the likeness of his son.* This is the purpose of our lives.

Therefore, if I am reading Paul correctly, all the craziness and apparent disconnections that have punctuated my life's journey as pastor, father, lover, and human being ultimately do connect. The *connection* is the creation of the image of Christ within me that these events have helped produce.

Paul says earlier in Romans 8, "I consider that our present sufferings are not worth comparing with the glory that will be revealed in us" (8:18). These present sufferings are apparently part of the bigger picture of the glory just described. Such is the substance of hope and the motivation to look to God that is the meaning of prayer. Accordingly, prayer and spiritual formation are appropriate final subjects of my story.

We all ask Alfie, the confidant in Burt Bacharach's popular song, "What's it all about? Is it just for the moment we live?"[2] Prayer and spiritual formation point the way to these answers. So, in this integrating moment, I will attempt to explain my position when it comes to giving and receiving prayer.

First, I will describe a unique experience I had with a parishioner that opened creative windows to spiritual formation and awareness. Second, I will discuss the problem of receiving intercession. Finally, I will describe persons who in unique ways have become companions with me in my spiritual journey.

A NEW WINDOW OF PRAYER

Creative Prayer and Cancer

Early in 1993, one of my parishioners received news from her doctor that she had a second onset of ovarian cancer. Understandably, this person was very distressed, and she came to me for something she could not get from the medical team that was working with her. That something she wanted was prayer. She had a twofold reason for coming that was more than her desire to be healed. First, she wanted to have the assurance that I as her pastor was appealing to God on her behalf. Second, she did not want to face this crisis alone without a spiritual companion, so she came to me. This crisis prompted some creative action on my part that revealed new insights about the possibilities of intimacy with God.

During the last five years, I have made an intentional effort to improve the quality of and to quantify the time I spend in prayer. My purpose has been to cultivate personal spiritual growth. The inspiration to seek this spiritual growth came from a seminar conducted by

Dr. Eugene Peterson and from the related writings of such persons as Don Postema and Hans Urs von Balthasar. These writings and the presentation by Dr. Peterson became my catalyst for seeking a deeper spiritual relationship with God.[3] Nonetheless, my parishioner's crisis with cancer stretched the limits of this venture by opening a new window of prayer and offering a fresh experience of intimacy with God.

For purposes of this narrative, I will call my parishioner Dorothy. According to Dorothy, the prognosis for recovery from a second onset of ovarian cancer was not good. Most victims die from the disease. Despite such a depressing prognosis, I personally believe in the power of God to provide healing in response to our prayers. Thus, I sought for ways in which to encourage Dorothy and give her hope. When I wrestled with Dorothy's situation and groped for effective strategies to offer her help, I remembered the story of the scapegoat in Leviticus 16. Here is a summary of the story.

Upon the day of atonement (compensation for wrongdoing), Aaron offered two goats at the altar of the tabernacle that was the place of worship for the Hebrew people during the time of Moses. One of the goats was to be slaughtered for the sins of the people (Leviticus 16:9). The other goat, however, would remain alive. Aaron would lay both his hands on the live goat ". . . and confess over him all the iniquities of the people of Israel" (Leviticus 16:21, RSV). This second goat (scapegoat) would be sent away into the wilderness (Azazel), and the goat would carry away from the Hebrew nation all of the iniquities that had been confessed over it.[4]

When I reflected on this story, I thought of a way to reenact this ritual that would express our own congregational faith. The primary purpose would be to encourage Dorothy. Nevertheless, I involved everyone in our small church, and the needs of many became a part of this reenactment. Here is what happened.

On the Sunday following my inspiration to reenact Aaron's ritual, I told the Leviticus story of the scapegoat to the congregation. When the story concluded, I first asked Dorothy and then the rest of the congregation to write their needs for physical, emotional, and spiritual healing on slips of notepaper. I then asked them to fold these papers and leave them unsigned. The slips were then put in a larger envelope and sealed. When this was done, I told the parishioners how I planned to reenact the ritual of the scapegoat. This is what I did.

Following the Sunday worship service, I decided to fast twenty-four hours. The next day, I took the sealed packet of personal needs (Dorothy's was foremost), and I set out for the wilderness. My choice of wilderness would not be Aaron's desert. I would select from the beautiful locales surrounding the Northern California community of Crescent City where I serve as a church planter. Crescent City is just twenty-five miles south of the Oregon border, situated in a protected region of the Pacific coastline and Redwood National Park. The destination I chose was the Lake Earl Wildlife Area, a 1,200-acre tract of forest and sand dunes. I hiked into this refuge on a drizzly January afternoon, carrying the needs (sins) of my congregation as a symbolic scapegoat.

I found an isolated spot deep in this wilderness and spent the afternoon in prayer. I removed the packet of notes and lifted them over my head. I petitioned God to show mercy on those represented. Then, I prayed for Dorothy and asked God to heal the cancer.

Following the time of prayer, I dug a deep hole in one of the sand dunes, and there I buried all the needs, hurts, and cries for deliverance that were expressed on those little slips of paper. I refilled the hole and walked away. The sufferings and afflictions of my congregation were left behind in that Azazel (solitary place), and there they remain buried.

What Were the Outcomes?

A year has passed since I served as scapegoat for my parishioners. Dorothy is still alive (1998). She has had surgery, and tests in subsequent months indicate that the cancer may be controlled. Also, Dorothy has stated that she feels closer to God and has experienced an uncommon peace in the midst of her difficult ordeal. Other participants from the congregation testified of spiritual encouragement, resolution of crises, and a deepening sense of God's presence.

A NEW OPPORTUNITY FOR PRAYER
AND INTIMACY WITH GOD

Notwithstanding the blessings Dorothy and the congregation received, I was deeply affected by this experience. I realized through the reenactment of the scapegoat story that I could benefit from a new pattern for prayer which the drama revealed. Consequently, I have set aside Mondays as a day for the wilderness. Weather and other circumstances do not always permit this retreat, but generally, in the early afternoon, I ride my bicycle out to the Lake Earl Wildlife Area and walk three miles into the preserve for a time of solitude, meditation, and prayer.

My Monday rendezvous is a different spot from where the scapegoat petitions are buried. The new setting is a sea of rolling sand dunes to which I am the lone visitor. The Siskiyou Mountains form a panorama to the east, and sounds of the Pacific surf crash distantly in the west.

These Mondays away have become a time of relaxation and meditation. I contemplate God's grace and mercy. The solitude and the wilderness place distance between me and the petty irritations and supposed crises of daily living.

The majesty of the Siskiyous reminds me that there is more to the story than my limited life. The surprising whir of a hundred seagulls beating the air in sudden flight above me makes the significance of my life seem even smaller. So too does the red ant, as it struggles over the grains of sand on the ridge of the dune, declare that the big picture of God's creative presence is larger than we suppose it to be.

The words God spoke to Job come to mind when I take time to walk barefoot in these solitary dunes feeling the warm sand filter between my toes:

Where were you when I laid the foundation of the earth?

Or who shut in the sea with doors, when it burst forth from the womb?

Have you commanded the morning since your days began?

Can you bind the chains of Pleiades, or loose the cords of Orion?

Is it by your wisdom that the hawk soars? Is it at your command that the eagle mounts up and makes his nest on high? (Job 38:4, 8, 12, 31; 39:26-27, RSV)

At length, when Job saw this larger picture God presented to him, Job said, "I . . . repent in dust and ashes" (Job 42:6, RSV). Likewise, I have been humbled by the greatness of God that I see in nature.

What Does Time Alone on a Sand Dune Have to Do with the Pastor and His Family?

The time alone on the sand dune is time alone with God. This window, through which I make more "space for God," has also helped me to slow down and make more room for my family. The solitude teaches me the value of making time for my family.

Bill Hybels echoes such sentiments in his book, *Too Busy Not to Pray:*

> God's power can change circumstances and relationships. It can help us face life's daily struggles. It can heal psychological and physical problems, remove marriage obstructions, meet financial needs—in fact it can handle any kind of difficulty, dilemma or discouragement.[5]

I believe prayer accomplishes the things Hybels says it will achieve because to those who pray a bigger picture of God is revealed. The exposure to this bigger picture slows us down, and this picture along with the discipline of prayer restructures our thinking and makes us more in tune with the rhythms and guidance of the Holy Spirit.

Similar to Hybels, Peter Wagner encourages the pastor to set aside time for dedicated prayer. Wagner, who maintains a focus on the growth and expansion of churches, realizes that the fulfillment of the mission of God does not occur for a person if that person is not willing to set aside time alone with God. Here is what Wagner says:

> Prayer is the chief way we express our love to God and the chief way we receive God's love for us . . .
>
> A central purpose in the kingdom of God is the multiplication and the growth of Christian churches, and we know that prayer is a chief instrument for releasing God's purposes into reality.[6]

Reflecting on Peter Wagner's assertion, God continues to impress upon me the importance of these windows of solitude and prayer, and

I seek to be faithful to these promptings. Further, I have found an additional window of prayer to be valuable. I used to meet with a minister from another denomination on Thursday mornings. We prayed for the community, for each other, our respective churches, and for other churches and pastors. We also attempted to engage in "warfare" prayer by petitioning God for the downfall of demonic spiritual strongholds that affect the region where we live. This prayer fellowship between me and this colleague was meaningful, but more important, I have recognized the necessity of receiving intercession as an outcome of our giving each other mutual support.

PERSONAL INTERCESSORS

Peter Wagner contends, "The most underutilized source of power in our churches today is intercession for Christian leaders."[7] Dr. Wagner lists these reasons for the underutilization of intercessors:

1. Ignorance of what the role of intercession is.
2. The problem of rugged individualism (I'll do it myself).
3. Fear of opening oneself up to another, especially as a pastor.
4. Spiritual arrogance.
5. Undue humility (I as a minister should not receive greater blessings than my congregation does).[8]

Finally, Wagner maintains that the pastor must learn to lay these objections aside and allow people to pray for him/her:

> I feel that a full appreciation of the operation of the body of Christ is a vital key to ridding ourselves of the obstacles that are in the way of receiving personal intercession.
>
> Intercessors may not be very visible, but they are like glands in the body that, 24 hours a day, secrete the hormones we need for life, health and energy.[9]

What Is Intercession?

Intercession is translated from a New Testament Greek term, *entugksano,* which means "to meet with, to come between." The

Hebrew equivalent in the Old Testament is *paga,* which means "to come or fall upon, to meet." A primary use of this term is found in Romans 8, where it describes the role of the Holy Spirit, who helps us maintain our faith and courage to live for God:

> Likewise the Spirit helps us in our weakness; for we do not know how to pray as we ought, but the Spirit himself intercedes for us with sighs too deep for words. And he who searches the hearts of men knows what is the mind of the Spirit, because the Spirit intercedes for the saints according to the will of God. (Romans 8: 26-27, RSV)

Peter Wagner upholds the human role of intercession:

> Intercession is the act of pleading by one who in God's sight has a right to do so in order to obtain mercy for one in need.[10]

Wagner goes on to illustrate the role of human intercession by offering biblical examples:

> Esther risked her life to plead on behalf of her Jewish counterparts when she went before Ahasuerus (Esther 4:16).
> Moses interceded for Joshua in the battles of Rephedim (Exodus 17).
> Further, Aaron and Hur held up the hands of Moses and assisted him in his act of intercession thus becoming intercessors for the intercessor.[11] (Exodus 17:8-13)

Wagner then cites New Testament examples of intercession. Jesus Christ stands in the gap for the people of God in John 17. James 5:16 encourages us to pray for one another. Finally, Paul requested personal intercession at least five times.[12]

My Search for Personal Intercessors

Peter Wagner further convinced me of the need for receiving intercession in two stories he told in Chapter 3 of *Prayer Shield.* The first was related by John Vaughan, a church growth leader, who was flying from Detroit to Boston where he was to conduct a pastor's seminar. According to Vaughan, a man seated next to him on the plane bowed his head and moved his lips in what appeared to be a prayer. Vaughan asked the man if he was a Christian. The man replied, "Oh, no. You have me all wrong. I'm not a Christian, I'm actually a satanist! . . . My primary attention is directed toward the fall of Christian pastors and their families living in New England."[13] Second, Wagner relates the story by Bill MacRae, who is chancellor of Ontario Bible College and Ontario Theological Seminary. MacRae stated that when he had been pastor of North Park Community Chapel in London, Ontario, he was told that there were satanists in his community who were praying for the elimination of evangelical leaders through marriage and family breakdown. On one occasion, MacRae went into a restaurant and observed a group praying in a corner booth. MacRae introduced himself as a fellow Christian, but the individuals "identified themselves as members of the church of Satan" who were praying for the destruction of a certain pastor in the community.[14]

These are contemporary confirmations that the Christian church and its ministers are engaged in serious spiritual warfare. If I heed this evidence, I discern that I cannot engage in ministry as an isolated individual. Not only do I need the support of my congregation and denomination, I also comprehend the need for personal intercessors.

Given this, I believe some of the suffering my family has experienced might have been alleviated if I had reached out sooner for personal intercessors. I seek such support now, but intercessors are not easy to find.

Levels of Intercession

Peter Wagner lists three groups of intercessors, and the taxonomy describes the closeness of relationship between the intercessor and the pastor. I will present Peter Wagner's classification and attempt to identify how his descriptions fit my own experience.

The most distant level in this classification is the *I-3 intercessor.* Wagner describes this intercessor as follows:

> I-3 intercessors can be quite remote from the pastor or the leader they pray for. Most I-3 intercession is a one-way relationship. The leader often does not know who the I-3 intercessor is or that he or she is praying for them and their ministry.[15]

My experience with I-3 intercessors parallels Wagner's description. I don't know all the persons who may be fulfilling this role. I occasionally find an I-3 intercessor through an unexpected letter or a chance meeting with certain persons who have said they pray for me. Other than these encounters, such persons remain anonymous.

I-2 intercessors are the next category. According to Wagner, I-2 intercessors have a regular but somewhat casual contact with the pastor or leader for whom they pray. The intercessors and the pastor "may cross paths from time to time in church related events. But for many, this is about the extent of personal contact."[16]

Three persons could be identified as my I-2 intercessors. The first is a colleague who has committed to pray for me. The second and third I-2 contacts are a couple who were part of a previous congregation. The couple have become my friends, and I believe they function as I-2 intercessors.

Finally, the closest intercessor is the *I-1 intercessor.* Here is Wagner's description:

> God calls I-1 intercessors to have a special, close relationship with the pastor or other leader. Sometimes this involves a close social relationship; sometimes it is largely a spiritual relationship. Most, if not all, of the I-1 intercessors I know have the gift of intercession.[17]

Whether I have an I-1 intercessor has been difficult for me to determine. For example, not too long ago, I assumed a certain person could likely be an I-1 intercessor. However, I was soon to discover that the relationship with this person had some dangerous aspects, and I backed away from the contact.

In support of my decision to retreat from an uncomfortable association, Peter Wagner's chapter, "Recruiting Prayer Partners," cautions pastors in the selection of intercessors. In the section, "Filtering Out the Flakes," Wagner says a warning that you may be getting associated with a flaky intercessor is shown by the desire of such a person to control you or manipulate you. Here is an illustration:

> Cindy Jacobs tells of "Estelle," whose prayer group "began to pray fervently that the pastor would 'see the light and get aligned with God'—which was synonymous with getting aligned with them." Estelle's mistake, Cindy says, was that "She felt her

'revelations' were superior to what the pastor or elders heard from God." She then goes on to explain how this tendency can be labeled an "Abasalom spirit." Need for control is dangerous and should not be tolerated in a prayer partner if it ever arises.[18]

For the reasons just described, I abandoned a prospective I-1 intercessor. With this person eliminated, I have sought to determine who my I-1 intercessors might be.

As I have considered the matter, I would conclude that my wife is my most important I-1 intercessor. First, she is a woman, and according to Peter Wagner, more women appear to have the gift of intercession than men. Second, Diana has demonstrated the gift of intercession in the following ways:

1. She doesn't desire to showcase her gift. She prefers to pray anonymously.
2. She prays for hours.
3. She receives supernatural revelation. (For example, Diana will sense a deep need to pray for our son and will subsequently discover he has been going through a difficult period that needed her intercession.)
4. Diana cares about my integrity and effectiveness as a minister.
5. Diana desires to pray.

Diana and I share intimately in the work of the ministry, and more than once I have been protected from making serious mistakes because of her wise insights and warnings. Diana is a very capable and stable I-1 intercessor.

THE SEARCH FOR A SPIRITUAL DIRECTOR

Eugene Peterson compares the life of a minister to that of a doctor. The doctor is entrusted with the care of physical bodies, while the minister is entrusted with the care of souls. Peterson cites this epigram that circulates among doctors: "A doctor who is his own doctor has a fool for a doctor." Similarly, "A pastor who is his own pastor has a fool for a pastor."[19]

Peterson argues that there are many reasons why pastors can't nurture themselves. One of these reasons concerns ego and spiritual pride. Another is the capacity in self-deceit in all of us that makes it almost impossible to see ourselves and our world from an objective point of view. Still another reason, says Peterson, is the discipline of subjection. Since we are "slaves" to the gospel, a spiritual director can teach us about obedience and what it means to be a servant who is answerable to someone else.[20]

In summary, we have a need to be accountable to someone because our human weaknesses will lead us astray. Peterson quotes John Cardinal Bona to punctuate his belief in our need for spiritual direction:

> Everybody should know this truth that no one is gifted with such prudence and wisdom as to be adequate for himself in the guidance of his own spiritual life. Self-love is a blind guide and fools many. The light of our own judgment is weak, and we cannot envision all dangers or snares or errors to which we are prone in the life of the spirit.[21]

Peterson cites other qualities of a good spiritual director that make such a person an indispensable asset to our spiritual formation. A spiritual director is more than a friend and offers more than comfort, emotional support, and religious chatter. A spiritual director, says Peterson, "has agreed to pay attention to my spiritual condition with me." For this reason alone, the search for a spiritual director can be difficult, and the seeker must be cautious.[22]

I will explore this subject further, but before I do, I will attempt to distinguish the differences between the role of a personal intercessor as described by Peter Wagner and the role of a spiritual director as described by Eugene Peterson.

The Difference Between an Intercessor and a Spiritual Director

Wagner's concept of the I-1 intercessor has *some* role overlap with Peterson's concept of a spiritual director. As with the spiritual director, the I-1 intercessor knows the pastor intimately. The I-1 intercessor has knowledge of weaknesses, concerns, and other facets of the pastor's life that the I-1 intercessor has not shared publicly. The I-1 intercessor engages in frequent dialogue with the pastor, and on the spiritual-ministerial level, this intercessor could know the minister as well as the spouse does.[23] Nevertheless, I think there are differences between Wagner's I-1 intercessor and Peterson's spiritual director. As a result, a pastor will ideally have both an I-1 intercessor *and* a spiritual director. Here are some distinctive characteristics of these spiritual roles.

The role of the I-1 intercessor is primarily supportive and subservient to the pastor. The purpose of the intercessor is to pray and be a spiritual go-between for the minister. Peter Wagner cautions that an I-1 intercessor is not to attempt to control the minister.[24] In contrast, Eugene Peterson contends that the role of a spiritual director is authoritative. The spiritual director offers guidance to a directee. Peterson concurs that spiritual directors should not be preoccupied with controlling another person. Nevertheless, by Peterson's definition, a spiritual director is not subservient to the directee.

Eugene Peterson defines a spiritual director as a special person who will take the time to listen and pay attention to the spiritual condition of another. Peterson describes outstanding qualities of his own spiritual director:

> Since this person has agreed to pay attention to my spiritual condition with me, I no longer feel solely responsible for watching over it. Now that someone experienced in assessing health and pathology in the life of faith is there to tell me if I am coming off the wall, I quit weighing and evaluating every nuance of attitude and behavior.[25]

As we continue to examine the difference between an intercessor and spiritual director, the possibility of these separate roles can be seen in Moses' life and experience. First, Aaron and Hur seem to have the role of intercessors. They held up Moses' hands so Israel would prevail in the battle against Amalek at Rephidim (Exodus 17). On the other hand, Jethro (Moses' father-in-law) appears to take the role of a guide or director. Jethro chides and corrects Moses for the way he judges the people. Then Jethro advises Moses to divide his workload and responsibilities with other capable men. Further, Moses did obeisance to Jethro that he did not do to Aaron and Hur (Exodus 18).

In summary, Jethro appears to fit Peterson's model of a spiritual director while Aaron and Hur appear to fit the model of Wagner's I-1 intercessor.

My Search for a Spiritual Director

Without question, a Jethro is a necessary asset for spiritual guidance. Notwithstanding, the search to find the right Jethro and a genuine Jethro is difficult. One of the barriers is fear.

Eugene Peterson remembers his own fears of letting someone into his spiritual space. He remembers thinking, "I can do it myself." Also, Peterson had an aversion to allowing anyone to exercise authority over him.[26]

I have these identical struggles, but there is another issue that makes choosing a spiritual director difficult for me. Since I was raised by alcoholics, I carry with me the numerous emotional weaknesses of other adult children of alcoholics. One of these weaknesses has been to subconsciously seek the "lost parent" in projected authority figures. As a result, I have not used good judgment in the past when I have chosen such authorities. My biggest problem has been not knowing my boundaries in relation to the boundaries of an authority figure.[27]

As I analyzed these past encounters with authority, I concluded that two things happened. First, I allowed inappropriate persons to exercise too much authority in my life while I played the role of the "good son." Second, I reacted to another extreme by shutting out appropriate authority figures with intense hostility. This behavior may be related to the shame I felt for giving the wrong people power to manipulate me. Consequently, the defense against allowing such abuse to happen again is to put everyone at arm's length.

Despite these past negative experiences, I now feel I know my boundaries. Hence, I believe I can make a good choice for a spiritual director. However, there is another barrier. Where does one find a guide who has the time?

Peter Wagner stresses that most spiritual leaders in evangelical circles are simply overburdened and overworked.[28] I know this to be the case in my own denomination. The chain of command in my denomination places the Director of Missions in the role of pastor to the pastors. Nevertheless, through no fault of his own or the denomination's, his supervision is divided too many ways. Not only does he care for thirty-plus pastors in addition to myself, the Director of Missions also carries a multitude of administrative duties. This person also lives three hundred miles away. At best, we have periodic contact by telephone. Intense spiritual direction is not something my Director of Missions is in a position to offer.

Because of the circumstances I have just described, I am seeking to find someone else who has the time and willingness to "pay attention to my spiritual condition with me." However, I have yet to find a person to fill this role. Those whom I have sought to fill this role have proved ineffective.

Washouts: Ineffective Spiritual Directors

Eugene Peterson recounts George Fox's encounters with five pastors who had their chance to provide him with spiritual direction. None of these five provided the needed help. Similarily,, I experienced at least three fruitless engagements that paralleled Fox's list.

The first was a minister who offered excellent insight but, unfortunately, he was intolerant of any of my ideas or experiences that did not fit his worldview. This person invalidated any experiences or dialogue which did not meet his terms or which he could not control. George Fox's equivalent spiritual director was the "Ancient Priest at Mancetter." Peterson comments about this comforter as follows:

> The ancient priest at Mancetter is a clerk in an ecclesiastical drugstore. He has a stock of folk wisdom that he mixes with churchy admonition and then dispenses like an apothecary.
> . . . The problem was not only in his advice but also the intent with which he gave it. He reveals his motives when he gets angry at Fox's refusal to buy. Fox, a stubborn customer, refuses the prescribed medication. That constitutes rejection for the priest.[29]

The second washout actually started out quite well. I arranged weekly phone contact with this person, and my hope was to unburden some intense personal struggles by working with this individual. Despite my efforts, the spiritual candor I sought to establish with this person never materialized. Besides this person's apparent inability to understand the purpose and content of my communication, he withdrew from intimacy when he realized that the dialogue I sought to establish with him would become too open and that he would become vulnerable. Consequently, because of fear and a desire to play the cards of his own life close so no one else could see, the possibility for spiritual direction evaporated. George Fox titled his equivalent experience "Priest Living About Tamworth." Peterson described this "hollow cask" as follows:

> If we are unprepared to engage in honest, open, shared inquiry after God, then we are of no use: "an empty hollow cask."
> . . . We devise stratagems and roles that allow us to function smoothly and successfully, without pain, anguish, and undue expenditure of psychic energy. But none of this can be sustained in an acutely personal spiritual encounter.[30]

The third washout was a problem solver. This person could not just listen; the individual had to come up with quick fixes and a resolution for every crisis. This friend could have been invaluable if he only had taken the time to listen. Fox's parallel comforter was "One Macham." Peterson had this to say about him:

> Macham is an activist . . . something has to be *done*. No matter what, *do* something . . .
> The suggestion to *do* something is nearly always inappropriate, for persons who come for spiritual direction are troubled over some disorder or dissatisfaction in *being*, not *doing*. They need a friend who will pay attention to who they are, not a project manager who will order additional busywork.[31]

A fourth disappointment for me was not on Fox's list. This person was a peer who had the capacity to offer support and direction. Notwithstanding, this individual was caught up in a quest to become famous and successful. These dreams are destructive when other callings and gifts become subservient to the passion for notoriety. Thus, my peer could be of no help. His quest to make his mark drowned his potential to be a spiritual director.

Encouragers

Despite the difficulties in attempting to find a person or persons to pay attention to my personal spiritual development, there have been some who have offered comfort and companionship in a special way.

Archer Torrey has been one of the first and most consistent of friends who has offered comfort and support. I first met Archer Torrey in the summer of 1963. He was on a missionary furlough from Korea. We met at Camp Noel Porter near Lake Tahoe in California. Though this meeting occurred over thirty years ago, Archer left me with some unforgettable memories.

Archer is an Episcopal priest who practiced early on the spiritual disciplines of prayer and meditation. I was also impressed by his dedication to correspond with 1,700 people a year to whom he offered encouragement and his time. Archer extended his friendship when we first met in the summer of 1963. I was not yet a Christian so he took the role of evangelist and facilitated my conversion that same summer.

We were to meet again in September 1963, when I enrolled at the University of Hawaii. Because Archer remembered that I would be attending the University of Hawaii and because he paid attention, he was the first person to greet me when I arrived in Honolulu. Archer was on his way back to Korea. He was returning home on the Pacific and Orient Lines ship, Oronsay, which made a port call in Honolulu. Through providence, I arrived in Honolulu the same day Archer's ship arrived. This was not preplanned. Archer left a note at my dormitory, and that evening, I had dinner with him on the ship. Following the meal, we had a special time of prayer and fellowship, and then we parted. What a miraculous day!

Since these memorable encounters, I have maintained correspondence with Archer Torrey over the last thirty years. I also made a pilgrimage to Kangwondo, Korea, in 1976, to visit Archer and Jesus Abbey, which is his place of ministry. Most recently, Archer was on furlough again in 1990, and we spoke for about an hour by phone when he stopped over in San Francisco.

Distance and our different callings have prevented Archer from being a fully focused spiritual director. Nevertheless, through our periods of contact and comradeship I received not only friendship, but also wisdom and perspective that has shaped who I have become. Archer Torrey deserves my love and respect; he has given me valuable guidance.

J. Kenneth Eakins is another person who has offered encouragement and who has paid attention to my spiritual development. I first

met Dr. Eakins when he was my Old Testament professor at Golden
Gate Baptist Theological Seminary in Mill Valley, California. We had
further contact through the readiness for ministry assessment that he
administered. Although his involvement in my spiritual development
began with these contacts, a deeper kinship evolved, and Dr. Eakins
became a friend and formative influence in the ensuing years.

Dr. Eakins officiated at my ordination in 1984, and we have kept
in touch with each other in subsequent years. Though distance and
the demands of our respective schedules have limited the contact,
Dr. Eakins has continued to show a dedicated interest in my spiritual
development.

Dr. Eakins emulates the following qualities of a good spiritual director, as described by Eugene Peterson:

> In my meetings with my spiritual director, I have often had the
> sense of being drawn into a living, oral tradition. I am in touch
> with a pool of wisdom and insight in the life of faith and the
> practice of prayer in a way different from when I am alone in
> my study. . . . In spiritual direction, I am guided to attend to my
> uniqueness in the large context and discern more precisely
> where my faith development fits on the horizon of judgment
> and grace.[32]

Dr. Eakins has broadened my experience and awareness in a similar
manner.

Third, Emil Authelet has been a most significant support and
spiritual director for me. Dr. Authelet has written the foreword to
The Pastor's Family. Although his schedule is very tight, and the
demands on his time are intense, Emil takes time to talk and share
burdens. His unique quality is his ability to hear what I say and not
attempt to gloss over the difficult experiences. Emil understands
through his own life experiences, that many of the troubles we
experience are difficult to understand and defy simplistic solutions.
Instead of offering simplistic solutions, Emil will just listen, and if
necessary, weep with me rather than force a resolution to an experience of distress (Romans 12:15). The other thing I appreciate about
Emil is his deep understanding of human weakness and failure that
have created much of the suffering we bear in this world. Nonetheless, Emil retains deep faith that the Christ who spilled his blood

and gave his life for humankind will ultimately rescue the race from the sorrow and suffering that is an ever-present wake in the river of human history.

Finally, there is David Zaslow. We have been out of touch in recent years; nevertheless, he was a point of light for me in the early 1990s. David Zaslow is a rabbi from Ashland, Oregon, who once assisted with worship and pastoral care for Temple Beth Shalom in Crescent City, California. Though we are apart on the messiahship of Christ, David shares the same passionate love for Elohim, God of both Christians and Jews.

David has provided for me tremendous insight into the message of the Old Testament as seen from a Jewish perspective. His faith in the presence and power of God is also an inspiration. When I formerly attended the services at Temple Beth Shalom, I went as a worshipper, to participate in the joy and pageantry of Jewish ritual. I listened afresh when David explored scripture from his unique heritage, and from David I gained insight into the Jewish tradition that is the superstructure of Christ's message and ministry.

During the spring of 1993, I attended a Shvuot service with David and his Jewish community in Ashland. The Shvuot service is a celebration of Pentecost on the day in which Moses received the Ten Commandments on Mt. Sinai. The purpose of the Shvuot is to wait on God for revelation in the same manner that Moses waited before God on Mt. Sinai. The Jewish ceremony is an all-night prayer vigil that includes singing, dancing, supplication, and a feast.

I prayed the whole night with David and the members of his Ashland community, and words simply can't describe the bonding we as Gentile and Jew experienced. Further, I was uplifted by the dedication to spiritual disciplines of prayer and ritual worship that were a part of this evening.

The Shvuot ends with the reading and the passing of the Torah. The officiating rabbi first reads the selected scripture, and then the scroll is passed to each celebrant. The celebrants kiss the scroll as a sign of love and devotion to God and his Word. I will never forget the moment the scroll was passed to me. I, as a Gentile in this company of Jews, was accepted as a brother of faith. I further realized during this very special moment that we Christians and Jews are connected together in unique ways that are both mysterious and sublime.

Possibly, you can see from this story how valuable the spiritual kinship with David Zaslow has been for me. Also, we wrote an interview together that was published by *The Other Side* magazine in January 1994. The title of the article is "Branches on the Same Tree." In this interview, we explore the common roots of our respective faiths.

MY FAMILY AND SPIRITUAL GROWTH

My spiritual pilgrimage is a personal journey to understanding, communion, and peace with God. Consequently, what choices I have made for my journey, I have not imposed on the rest of my family. Edwin Friedman speaks of uniqueness and separateness of family members as a sign of a healthy relationship. With this in mind, I realize that my role is not to be the spiritual cop for any other family member.

My choices for spiritual development are just that: my choices. Other members of the family by right may take the route each chooses for spiritual development: Diana has the gift of intercession, and her time alone with God, though different in style and interval is appropriate to her spiritual journey. Likewise, my daughter has again another format of spiritual growth. She reads Christian novels with a devotional emphasis. Finally, my son finds his time alone through intentional retreats to isolated mountain settings. His love for nature coupled with a personal need for solitude is his preferred way to pray.

What I have to offer my family is not the designing of their spirituality. Instead, my family receives from me my commitment to pay attention to God and cultivate my own spiritual growth. As I pay attention to God, I learn how to love and serve them.

Chapter 11

Setbacks, Heartbreaks, and New Opportunities

When *The Pastor's Family* was reviewed by The Haworth Press, the editor noted that the Preface spoke of events that were not discussed in the first ten chapters. Consequently, I was asked to expand upon these events to fill in "a significant gap" in our story. I also thought about some other issues I wanted to address to round out the picture of this life of a family who loves God, one another, and has expressed desires for personal and conjoint excellence.

This will be a stream of consciousness journey. Nonetheless, these events will be touched upon:

1. Our journey through both a physical and spiritual desert
2. A near-bankruptcy and period of homelessness
3. My father's death
4. Further setbacks, surprises, and adjustments
5. Adversity that became a door of opportunity
6. Diana's self-actualization
7. Our children as adults
8. A reflection on pastoral ministry from the back pew

I plan to punctuate these events with both published and unpublished writings that I composed during the times these life-passages occurred. I am not sure where we will end up, but here it goes.

THE ORIGINAL SETTING

The early locale for events in *The Pastor's Family* was a pastorate in a rural, Southern Baptist church in Gualala, California. Gualala is a small community perched on the bluffs of southern Mendocino County, overlooking the Pacific Ocean. We began our term of service in this community on August 12, 1983, and we left on May 28, 1989.

Gualala and southern Mendocino County, despite pressures of development, still remain idyllic with the Pacific Ocean, California redwoods, wildlife, and steelhead-rich rivers providing the ambiance. Nonetheless, making a living for our growing family proved to be a major challenge as the church could only provide limited support. Therefore, in an effort to establish a viable financial base, we pursued the activities I described in Chapter 1. These activities included the establishment of a bookstore and office supply, which we called Mendocino Mercantile. Additionally, I developed a business as an independent sales representative for various gift manufacturers and distributors. Through these efforts, we were able to establish ourselves in the community, buy a home, and become part of life as it was lived in this remote corner of California. Despite the stresses on our family life due to the heavy schedule and the days I spent on the road, we could have lived in Gualala much longer than we did. Diana loved her home and the beautiful environment.

Nevertheless, I was restless. We began the ministry in Gualala when I was in my early forties, and I was not satisfied that this place was to be our first and only tenure of ministry. I was looking for other mountains to climb. The opportunity for the next quest arrived in the fall of 1987. I attended a church growth institute at Robert Schuller's Crystal Cathedral (Garden Grove, California) and met Peter Wagner from Fuller Theological Seminary who was conducting one of the workshops at this institute. He spoke of opportunities to earn a Doctor of Ministry degree from Fuller, and I was immediately interested. I mailed a completed application a few weeks later and was ultimately accepted into the program. The first seminar began in the spring of 1988.

I look back on the years I attended Fuller as some of the best for both Diana and me. This book is the essence of that Fuller experience. Diana and I attended all of the seminars together. We discovered what we needed to do to heal our marriage and family life as a result of our experience in Arch Hart's "Minister's Personal Growth and Skill Development Workshop."[1] The insights on spirituality as described in Chapter 10 were gleaned in part from the seminar "Spirituality and Ministry" by Eugene Peterson[2] and "Healing Ministry in the Local Church" by Peter Wagner.[3] Most important, *The Pastor's Family* was the subject of my dissertation for the completion of the degree. For all of these things, I am indebted to Fuller Theological Seminary.

Concurrently, there was another aspect of the Fuller experience that contributed to my spiritual journey in some very unexpected ways. I enrolled at Fuller Seminary primarily to gain all possible knowledge about church growth. I attended every seminar available on the theory and application of church growth principles. I sat under the tutelage of John Wimber and Peter Wagner. I devoured books and tapes on the subject and as a class project I evaluated a highly successful church in Southern California. I still believe in the value and importance of church growth as taught by the best of the best in the field. Nevertheless, my dream to become a highly successful church growth-oriented pastor/planter led me through a physical and spiritual desert. These experiences created turmoil and caused major changes in our lives. Nonetheless, the events produced unexpected spiritual insights that I was not prepared to embrace at first, but have come to understand as another side to the church growth vision.

The emphasis of church growth as I have understood it includes a pastor who has three qualities:

1. The pastor wants a church to grow.
2. The pastor is willing to assume the responsibility for growth.
3. The pastor is willing to enlist lay people and share the ministry with them.[4]

I believed I had these qualities and could create a new church with multitudes of excited and happy people. Publicity is a piece of cake. I could communicate a vision. I could inspire enthusiasm. I could motivate people to serve God. Consequently, as a result of this side of my training at Fuller, I resolved in March 1989 to announce my resignation at Gualala Baptist Church and begin a church growth project. I submitted my resignation, and we made plans to leave Gualala and move to Southern California.

THE HEAT OF THE DESERT

Diana had been with me through all of the church growth work-shops, and she expressed mixed emotions about the whole concept. For one thing, Diana voiced great fear that she and the family would be swallowed up by another one of my projects, and she said, "I don't like this." Diana was also bothered by the "slick profession-alism" of some of the purported model churches, which struck her as being unauthentic. She wondered how the families of these pur-ported, successful ministers *really* felt about being a part of a mega-church and if such superpastors were attentive to their children and accountable to their spouses. Despite her misgivings, Diana, *again,* was willing to pay the price so that I could reach another goal. Maybe this was the final and most important lesson I was to learn. That lesson came packaged in the death of my church growth dream, followed by months of sorrow. Finally, I would be pushed to a situation in which Diana would at last have her turn to grow and fulfill her dreams.

We left Gualala on May 28, 1989. Our move went very smoothly. We were able to sell both our house and business, and we received a modest profit on these sales. Nevertheless, leaving was a time of grief for Diana. She loved the house we had lived in. She feared that she would never get another home, and this fear almost became a reality. With a heavy heart, yet a willingness to follow me, she packed her treasures, and we took them in a U-Haul to a storage unit near her mother's home in Rocklin, California. We then set out to find a place to start a new church.

One of the ideas gleaned from our church growth training was to find a community that was experiencing growth, so we chose to explore the high desert area of Southern California. We drove to Lancaster and Palmdale to check out the possibilities. We did this with no promise of support from the denomination we had been serving. I was going on an inspiration, and I hoped to enlist denomi-national support when Diana and I found a place to begin a new ministry. This new ministry did not materialize, and both we and the dream withered in the heat of the high desert summer.

Diana and I fought constantly on the trip to Palmdale and Lan-caster. Both of us realized that we were not accustomed to the severe summer heat of the Lancaster-Palmdale region after spending almost seven years on the cool north coast of California. We did not find any area in which we felt comfortable, and the price of housing was exhorbitant for what one received in a purchase. We explored the area for about a week, becoming more discouraged as our search went on. Finally, on the last day, Diana said, "Dan, I don't want to do this. We do not belong here. Dreams or not, this is not the place I want to start a church. Please, let's go." I agreed, and so ended, at least for that moment, the great plan I envisioned for a burgeoning church.

A LONG, DARK NIGHT OF WANDERING AND LOSS

We returned to Rocklin, California, the home of Viola West, Diana's mother. We told her that our plans to move to Southern California were scrapped and asked if we could stay with her for a few weeks. That few weeks became a year, and the back bedroom of Viola's house became our residence. The truth was that we were now homeless.

Truthfully, I was lost. I did not know what to do. I had been moving on a dream and an inspiration, but now there was no alternate plan to backup the abandonment of my new church aspirations. For one thing, I was getting very nervous about our finances. We had made a small profit on the sale of our house and business when we left Gualala, but that would soon be gone unless I found some kind of work. Diana and I discussed options, and we decided to open another bookstore and office supply in a shopping center across the street from Viola's home. We negotiated with the owners of the shopping center and in a few months opened Rocklin Books and Office Supply. The decision was made in an effort to make some sense out of the dead end we had found ourselves in. Once again, Diana saw my enthusiasm for restarting our former business, and she was willing to help because, as she later reflected, the plans gave me hope. What we were to encounter, however, was another deep disappointment. Contrary to our modest success in Gualala, Rocklin Books and Office Supply died a premature death from undercapitalization and a lack of customers. Thousands of our scarce dollars went to the grave with the business failure. These compounded losses were more painful than anything I had experienced in years. I was facing an abyss that held within two of my deepest fears: failure and financial ruin. I could not have imagined things getting any worse.

The deep pain of this loss was expressed in a story I wrote that appeared in *Decision* magazine in February 1994. In "Grace in an Unexpected Place" I described how my struggle with anger and bitterness was resolved.

After the business failed, I accepted a job as chaplain at an alcohol and drug recovery hospital. I attended A.A. (Alcoholics Anonymous) meetings as part of my duties, and at one of these meetings I experienced the comfort of God. As my turn to speak approached my eyes filled with tears.

> I looked intently at each participant as I said, "I have a story too. My problem is not drinking, but I have agonized just as you have. My business failed; I lost thousands of dollars; my family has suffered; I feel hopeless, and I too need recovery."
>
> They understood. We embraced, for we had discovered that we were as one. "The God of all comfort" was there for me in an unexpected way in that unexpected place.[5]

That story described, in part, a very dark spring and summer in 1990. I estimated that personal loss from the closure of our business was at least $20,000. We were as financially devasted as we could become. We had no home, our assets had vaporized, and we were in debt to creditors who were pressing for payment. I had considered filing for bankruptcy and had spoken with an attorney about this procedure. However, I decided against filing, and despite the pressure we encountered from our creditors, we were able to either pay off or bring all our accounts current within five years. Diana and I both consider this was achieved through the grace of God.

Parallel to the struggle and lack of direction we experienced during this dark season, a family crisis occurred in July 1990. My father was enjoying a day with my mother on the Yuba River in the Sierra Nevada Mountains when he suffered a stroke. My mother was able to summon help and got my father to a hospital in Truckee. My dad rallied briefly, but a second stroke took his life. He died on July 14, 1990.

When I wrote this chapter, I was especially interested in listening again to the eulogy I gave at my father's funeral. Besides telling some childhood anecdotes about myself and my brothers, I expressed that in addition to being the cocreator of my life, my father was also a framer of my philosophy of life. These connections run deep.

My dad was really sour on religion, and one time he told me that he did not believe in God because God did not answer his prayers. My dad also had a premonition when I was younger that I might become a minister, and this really bothered him. When I was about ten years old, either because of questions I had or a viewpoint I expressed, my dad said something like: "You remind me of Aimee Semple McPherson, and God help us if you become like her!" I don't know whether I was the feared reincarnation of Aimee Semple McPherson, but my father was very uncomfortable when I announced in my early twenties that I had made a personal dedication to Christ and planned to dedicate my life to God's service. My father eventually came to accept these choices, but I do not know if he ever changed his negative views of God.

Nevertheless, despite our apparent distance on some spiritual matters, I realized after my father's death that his view on life contributed to my spirituality. My father was a lover of nature. He respected and adored the creation that God bestowed upon us. At the same time, my father was very angry about the abuse of nature and the environment by human greed for wealth and power. I don't know if love and respect for nature and the environment are hereditary qualities, but I do know that my dad and I had almost identical views on the love of nature and protection of the environment. This worldview was a gift I received from him. I am amazed that my son shares these sentiments as well.

My father sought to relate to people on what could best be described as authentic interaction. He hated pretense. Similarly, I am repulsed by persons who are insincere and who are more concerned about image and reputation than being genuine in their relationships. Finally, my father was fascinated with life and its mysteries. One of the last conversations I had with him was on the subject of quarks, which are particles smaller than atoms. My father had been reading an article about quarks, and stated, "You know, Danny, the research they are doing on atoms now appears to show that the essence of all matter is nothing but vibrating energy." I don't remember if I said anything to my father at the time, but his description of that research into subatomic particles reminded me of two passages in the Bible. The first is Genesis 1:1-2, "In the beginning God CREATED the heavens and the earth. The earth was without form and void, and darkness was upon the face of the deep; and the Spirit of God was moving over the face of the waters" (RSV). This biblical description of the earth being without form and void was like the vibrating energy my father described. The second passage is in John 1:1, "In the beginning was the Word, and the Word was with God, and the Word was God" (RSV). The notes in the Oxford Bible state not only that Jesus is this "logos," but also that the Word (logos) is God in action.[6] I thought again of my father's awe of "vibrating energy" and the unique connection between this discovery of science and the action of The Word. Though by appearance we seemed eons apart, my father's spirituality influenced mine.

My dad was an extremely intelligent person. He graduated from the University of California at Berkeley with a Bachelor of Science in Forestry. He was a chemist and a master botanist. He also illustrated a children's book called *Chuffer*, the story of a little steam engine that refused to open its eyes when it was racing down the tracks. My father was a man of great achievement, and this all came to an end in this dark year of 1990. His death left much unfinished business in our relationship. This was a blend of his genius and creativity mixed with the negative effects that his use of alcohol played in his interactions with me, both as a child and adult. His death compounded the grief I was already experiencing with our business failure and apparent loss of direction for our lives.

The death of my father helped me realize that my life was intricately connected to his. I believe the same is true of my mother. My mother, who will soon be eighty years old, has an enthusiasm for life and people and she is an independent, active person. She has been socially involved with people and programs throughout her life, and has had a desire to help others and to contribute to positive social change in the communities where she has lived. I believe I am connected to these qualities expressed in my mother's life. Again, I do not know how much of this connection is hereditary, but she did provide the model of social involvement and concern for people that I strive to emulate.

A TRIP THAT CHANGED OUR DESTINY

It was in mid-August of 1990 that Diana spoke to me about trying something new.

She said, "Dan, we are getting nowhere staying in Rocklin and Sacramento. Let's see what else is out there. Let's just get in the car and start looking. We both agreed that we do not want to live where the heat is oppressive. Why don't we drive north and just see what happens."

We were penniless, so we asked our son, Dan Aaron, if we could borrow $300 from him to make this trip. He agreed, and we embarked on another life-changing journey. We drove to the San Francisco Bay Area and then north on Highway 101 toward Oregon and Washington. One of the first stops was Crescent City, California. It seemed to be a rambling, coastal town that was reminiscent of our days in Gualala. I asked Diana, "Would you like to live here?" She said, "Not really." Nevertheless, we picked up a local paper and sat in the car in a McDonald's parking lot and read the want ads. There was a job advertised for a teaching position at Del Norte High School. I decided that I might as well put in an application, so I found the district office and filled out the necessary paperwork.

We continued our journey that took us to Portland, Washington, Vancouver, and eventually, Seattle. Nothing promising appeared to open up in any of these cities, and we returned to Rocklin and Diana's mother's house wondering if our journey was another dead end. However, when we came in the door, Viola greeted us with the news that we had received a call from Crescent City and the Del Norte County School District. I was invited to an interview for a high school teaching position. The winds of hope again filled the sails of our beached ship of life. I had no idea if we would ever be in the ministry again, but at least with a teaching position, we could put food on the table and pay our bills. We drove back to Crescent City; I interviewed for the opening at the high school and was offered the job. Life was looking good again. Diana and I were so excited. We eagerly made plans for the move, not knowing that further disappointment and heartbreak awaited us.

HOPE FRUSTRATED AGAIN

I began teaching at Del Norte High School with renewed optimism that our season of troubles was over. Unfortunately, in a few weeks that optimism evaporated amidst new concerns and anxieties. Within a month after beginning the assignment, the principal, with pen and notebook in hand, started making regular visits to my classes. He would not say much, but he sat in the back of the room taking copious notes. About mid-October, I asked him if there was a problem. He assured me that I was doing a fine job, and his visits were part of a first-year evaluation process. My intuition told me something was wrong. Another thing I noticed was that the number of visits to my classes was considerably more than visits to the classes of the other new teachers.

The day before the Christmas break in 1990, the principal informed me that if my performance did not improve I would not have a job next year. I broke the news to Diana, and we spent a gloomy winter break wondering again what our future would hold.

I met with the principal in early January, 1991, I told him that I was perplexed that I did not receive an earlier warning that my job performance was unsatisfactory. "After all," I told him, "your statements were positive until you gave me your ultimatum before the winter break." Although he replied, he never offered a relevant explanation. The problem, according to California educational law, was that because of codes relating to tenure, a public school principal could fail to renew a contract for a teacher, "without cause" during the first two years of that teacher's employment.

I prepared for the worst, which did come. The assistant principal informed me shortly before the end of February that my teaching contract was terminated, and warned me that I had to teach through the end of the year or they would threaten to take away my teaching credential.

I appealed the decision to the point of having the district superintendent observe my class. Following a class visit, he stated that he thought I was doing a fine job, but he would not force the principal to keep me. However, it was in this final experience of darkness and despair that things began to turn around.

HOPE RENEWED

I do not believe that all negative experiences are God-ordained. Nonetheless, I have come to understand that seasons of darkness are just that—seasons. My despair did not last forever, and new opportunities unfolded following my termination from Del Norte High School. Marshall Loeb is one of many persons who cites that the Chinese characters for crisis mean "danger" and "opportunity."[7] Consequently, a crisis can be looked upon as a "dangerous opportunity." Concurrently, Roger von Oech says much the same thing when he describes adversity as a way of forcing you to see new opportunities that heretofore you would never consider.

Occasionally, we all need a jolt to shake us out of routine patterns, to force us to rethink our problems, and to stimulate us to ask the questions that may lead to other right answers.

"Jolts" come in all shapes, sizes, and colors. They have one thing in common, however; they force you—at least for the moment—to think of something different. Sometimes you'll get jolted by a problem or a failure. Sometimes it will be the result of a joke or a paradox. And sometimes it will be a surprise or an unexpected situation. "It could result from your getting fired from a job, or failing to obtain a performance raise."[8]

This was just such a crisis that brought an end to a long year of struggle and ultimately caused us to stumble through new doors of opportunity.

During the summer of 1991, following my dismissal from the high school, Diana responded to an advertisement for the position of Director of Staff Development at the Crescent City Convalescent Hospital. She was hired, and within a few years was promoted to Director of Nurses. Concurrently, Diana also found out about a continuing education program for a Bachelor of Science degree in Nursing at Humboldt State University in Arcata, California. She enrolled in this program in 1993, and in 1998, Diana received her Bachelor of Science in Nursing. This marvelous achievement has created opportunity for her to give to others in her profession. At least part of Diana's good fortune resulted from her actions following the loss of my job at the high school.

I also discovered opportunities I would not have considered if the misfortune of the job termination had not occurred. In the fall of 1991, since Diana was working there, I began making regular visits to the Crescent City Convalescent Center. I went to visit residents as a pastor and to give them time and attention. Within a month of my involvement with the nursing home residents, the director of the convalescent hospital asked if I would consider accepting a position as a Social Service Designee. I eagerly agreed to take the job and am currently working at the same facility.

I also had an opportunity to advance my education. California State University at Sacramento had begun an external degree program for the completion of a Master of Social Work degree. Classes were held at Shasta College, once a month on weekends, in Redding. The program was designed for full-time, rural workers to enable them to complete an MSW degree without having to give up employment. I began this program in the fall of 1993 and joyfully graduated in May 1996 with new credentials, new tools, and new opportunities in the service of others. I do not believe that I would have ever found these doors of opportunity if I had not experienced the adversity at the high school. One additional note: despite the negative encounter with Principal Claggart, an opportunity opened up to help develop an adult school program in the same district from which I was terminated. I am still employed as an adult school instructor and coordinator. The results of these labors have been very successful.

Romans 8:28 states the following about our lives as followers of Christ: "And we know that in all things God works for the good of those who love him, who have been called according to his purpose. Fo those God foreknew he also predestined to be conformed to the likeness of his Son, that he might be the firstborn among many brothers" (NIV). My theological perspective is such that I do not believe God creates evil circumstances to torment us (see James 1:13). I believe there are three players in our life story. God is one player. We, ourselves, are collectively the next player. The good and evil we do, the mistakes and poor judgments we make, all affect how life unfolds for us. Finally, I believe that Satan (the accuser/destroyer) is the third player. The evil that befalls us comes either from our own failures or the harrassment of our spiritual adversary, the devil (see 1 Peter 5:8).

Nevertheless, God somehow is able to turn our worst troubles into something good. This does not mean that we see immediate, Cinderella-like rescues from our dilemmas, but it does appear to me that God eventually reconciles the heartbreak and tragedies that befall our lives if we, in the spirit of Romans 8:28, are looking to God for deliverance from our troubles. This is the substance of the Lord's Prayer: ". . . And lead us not into temptation, But deliver us from evil" (Matthew 6:13, RSV).

Possibly, one of the secrets for finding this deliverance from God is to seek it. I have spoken to others about the problem of weeping and agonizing at a closed door of opportunity so much so that we are unable to see doors all around us that are wide open. My counsel to those who struggle with adversity is not to cry over barriers but seek out the unhindered gateway. Such is my conviction as I reflect on the good fortune that followed the very dark days we experienced in 1990.

A NEW OPPORTUNITY FOR MINISTRY

During the years I was pastor at Gualala Baptist Church, I became friends with Bob Rasmussen. Bob was the executive minister for The American Baptist Churches of the West until February 1997. He would vacation at the nearby Sea Ranch resort and coastal community with his wife Paula and friends, Floyd and Beverly Roseberry. Bob did lose touch with what had happened to us after we left Gualala in 1989. Nonetheless, he received news in the early summer of 1991 that I was in Crescent City. As a result, I received a call from his office in Oakland, California, asking if I would be interested in starting a new American Baptist Church in Crescent City. I jumped at this opportunity, and in August 1991, I was accepted as the new church planter for the area. The sponsorship of the project came from American Baptist churches in Eureka and Arcata, California, as well as Brookings, Oregon. I eagerly looked forward to the development of this new church, but some incredible twists and turns followed in this journey that made the outcome far different from my early expectations.

The first surprise came shortly after I began the project. I received a call from leaders in the Brookings church asking if I would fill in for a Sunday service. I wondered what had happened to their pastor. I was soon to discover that he had been arrested for molesting some children in his congregation. At that moment, I knew that this church planting project was going to be a roller-coaster ride. The Brookings church eventually called another pastor, but the new minister was hostile toward the church planting project and ultimately withdrew his support in a critical letter to the national headquarters of the denomination.

Nevertheless, I pressed on. The vision for this new church was to attract persons who were not already attending a church in Crescent City. The target population was prison guards, their families, and other employees at the new state prison. I had no significant contact with these persons, so the strategy used was to set up and advertise what could best be described as "felt need" groups since some of our target population may not be church attenders. Some of the groups I attempted to form included topics on codependency, stress, and attention deficit problems with children. I followed a format from a small group study series published by Serendipity Publishers. I was able to obtain meeting space at a local restaurant and a local bank. Overall, the six-week sessions on each topic were generally successful, attracting about ten people for each series. The idea behind the small groups was to develop a core of people who might be interested in starting a church. Though they showed interest in the workshops, none of these individuals ever became part of the new church.

Our next strategy was to attempt to make contact with people through both the radio and the local newspaper. We purchased space in the paper and time on the radio. I began a series of commentaries called "The Pastor's Notebook," which ran in the paper and aired on the radio generally once a week for about one year. The purpose of the series was to make the presence of the new church known and to attract people to the opening service. We were following a pattern that delayed the actual start of the church to first stimulate interest in the community. As just mentioned, I began work on the project in August 1991, but our first service did not commence until May 10, 1992.

Finally, as we set the target date for the first service, further attempts to advertise our presence were initiated. Participants from supporting churches and I rang doorbells and left flyers announcing the opening service. I also rented space in a local flea market as well as a booth in a spring home show to herald our opening worship service. The crowning touch to this media blitz was an announcement that went to every mailbox in Crescent City in a weekend advertiser published by the newspaper.

The opening service was on Mother's Day, 1992. We obtained space in an elementary school multipurpose room. However, the school district would only allow us to use the space for six weeks. The school district was very nervous about being connected to a religious body in the rental agreement and did not want to incur negative publicity. We had six weeks to find a more permanent location, so we looked forward to this birthing service. Leaders from the denomination, members of the new church steering committee, and about fifty visitors from the community took part in this inaugural, which got off to a great start until we heard loud banging at the back door of the multipurpose room. The service went on, but I soon discovered that an irate middle-aged lady, who drove up in a beat-up Volkswagon, yelled at the back door that a public school was no place for a church to hold a service, and she would see to it that we never met here again. She interrupted us twice and then cornered me at the end of the service, reiterating her threats. So, this was opening day for American Baptist Fellowship—a day full of unexpected and unwanted excitement.

We met for about three more weeks at the school. The lady never came back, but I knew that we would have to find another place. Predictably, our numbers dropped on the following Sunday. Part of the decline may have been due to the harangue we received from the protestor and part from the inevitable attrition of casual visitors. Ultimately, the numbers bottomed out to plus or minus fifteen—where the church attendance has remained to the present.

Our search for a permanent meeting place further tested the tenacity of the participants. We were offered a place in the Masonic Lodge, which sparked more controversy because the pastor at one of our sponsoring churches was incensed that we would even consider meeting there since Masons allegedly held occult beliefs. To compound the problem at the Masonic Lodge, we were originally promised a well-lighted dining area for our service. What we ended up with was the dark, windowless hall used for the lodge's ceremonies. Understandably, this further hampered our efforts to establish the fledgling church. Ultimately, we were able to find a permanent location at the Episcopal church in town who rented us their parish hall on Monday evenings. This is now the location of American Baptist Fellowship.

The following excerpt from an American Baptist newspaper, *The Planter,* summarizes all of the events that followed:

> What happened? The church was originally projected to reach prison guards at the newly constructed Pelican Bay State Prison. However, the guards did not respond. Instead, it was some of the poorest members of the community who were turning out. Yes, God did have a plan, and Daniel found himself as a pastor to the poor.
>
> Pastor Langford reflects, "The people who attend American Baptist Fellowship don't always fit into mainstream society. We as a church have described ourselves as 'poor in possessions but rich in faith.'" His congregation consists of welfare recipients, single parents, and an occasional homeless visitor.
>
> Langford, who has a doctorate from Fuller Seminary, sees ministering to the poor as the true gospel. "The world sees such people as 'nobodies,' but God sees them as precious," he says. "I have to work two jobs to allow me to serve as an unpaid pastor, but God will not give up on these people, so neither will I. Mother Teresa said it best, 'I wasn't called to be successful; I was called to be faithful.' "[9]

The hope that American Baptist Fellowship would become a burgeoning megachurch in Crescent City did not occur, and the dilemma I was faced with was whether or not to honor the request of a small band of powerless people who asked me to be their pastor. I would receive no denominational support if I chose to carry on the ministry because the rules were that the new church had to be able to maintain itself in three years. Nonetheless, I made the decsion not to abandon these people because their numbers were small and they were poor. I was willing to serve as an unpaid pastor, and I have not regretted this decision. The community that is being built will not elicit "oohs and aahs" on a statistical grid of numbers, money, and power. However, this community of believers is growing in other ways that appear to fit a New Testament model of spirituality, but not necessarily a business model of presumptuous success. I recently wrote down the qualities I found in the community of my small church. These are some of the reasons I know my efforts are not wasted.

The participants in the community of the American Baptist Fellowship collectively

1. demonstrate patience with one another,
2. express acceptance of the diversity in each member,
3. have a willingness to learn and be taught principles of spirituality as expressed in the Bible and especially the New Testament,
4. show love by paying attention to one another and sincerely praying for one another's needs,
5. disregard common social barriers of money and class by creating an environment of comfortable acceptance for all participants.

A BALANCED MINISTRY
AND A BALANCED FAMILY

When I look at life as I now experience it, I believe that the balance of giving time and attention to my marriage and family is better than it was in earlier years when I was preoccupied in the struggle for success. The sufferings and turmoil I experienced may have been ways God used to bring about this balance.

My Ministry is a more authentic expression of who I am. I look at my current situation, and I sincerely want to do the things I am doing. Pastoral care is not only occurring in the context of my church but also in the contexts of my employment:

- I am a pastor to the residents I serve as a social worker in the nursing home.
- I am a pastor to the adults from other countries to whom I teach English as a second language.
- I am a pastor to inmates at the county jail to whom I teach basic education skills.
- I am a pastor to the young men and women at the California Conservation Corps with whom I serve as a counselor.

My role as an encourager, comforter, and spiritual leader is not limited to the walls that define a church. I am happiest and feel most fulfilled in being able to express my faith, not only in the structure of the church, but also in the settings of life that make up the world outside the church. Jesus said, "Therefore go and make disciples of all nations . . . teaching them to obey everything I have commanded you" (Matthew 28:19-20, NIV). The diversity of my life and vocations makes the fulfillment of this commission a rich reality.

BALANCE IN MY MARRIAGE AND FAMILY

It would be wrong to say that I have straightened everything out in my marriage and relationships with my children. New challenges arise every day. Nevertheless, things continue to get better as I learn to let go more as my wife and children build their lives as differentiated individuals.[10]

Diana

Diana has made some courageous decisions that have improved not only her own life but our marriage as well. Diana is no longer a part of the work I do in pastoral ministry. She is supportive of my work, but she is pursuing her own life goals instead of being swallowed up by mine. Diana has two special gifts: one of them is intercessory prayer, and the other is a gift of leadership. She is using both gifts in her unique role as the Director of Nurses for Crescent City Convalescent Hospital. Though she may not spend the rest of her life at this nursing home, Diana has a passion to create an environment of dignity and quality care for aging adults and others requiring skilled nursing care. This passion not only includes direct contact with the nursing home resident but also the motivation of a caregiving team to do their very best for this group of people. Diana further advocates the causes of justice and dignity for nursing home residents outside the facility in the immediate community and beyond. She is also preparing to enter a master's program in nursing administration and hopes to someday teach principles of geriatric care at the college level.

It is okay that Diana has separated from the oft-smothering involvement with my goals and life as a minister. She has had to wrestle with personal guilt and the imagined raised eyebrows of those who still do not understand that individuals such as a husband and wife can be very spiritual, and at the same time, pursue very different journeys in the expression of that spirituality. My congregation has had to be instructed that Diana does not come as part of the minisrty package. Nonetheless, these are right and good decisions, and our personal relationship and overall effectiveness as helpers of people have significantly improved.

Dan Aaron

Since the time my story began, our son has grown into a twenty-five-year-old adult with a family of his own. He and his beloved partner, Kristie, gave us our first grandson, Daniel Shayne, of whom we are very proud. Probably the most difficult thing for me to learn has been to be a support for Dan Aaron during some difficult times in his life journey. As a parent, it is difficult to see our children experience pain, no matter how old the child might be. The temptation is to step in with unsolicited advice to try to fix our children's problems. Dan Aaron weathered an extremely stressful time because of some struggles he was having with educational achievement. He made a decision to seek help at a community college where he discovered he had high intelligence but also had a distinctive learning style that favored both auditory and tactile/kinesthetic modes of learning. Through the help of College of the Redwoods in Eureka, Dan Aaron discovered the strategies that would help him succeed with his learning style. He went on to enroll in the college's police academy, graduating fifth in a class of twenty-five. We are very proud of Dan Aaron who is now a sheriff's deputy in a small town in the northern Sierra Nevada mountains of California.

Deanna

I am amazed. Both of my children became law enforcement officers. It would be an interesting study to determine how their family of origin (being preacher's kids) affected these career choices. Deanna completed her Associate in Arts Degree at College of the Redwoods in 1997. She then entered basic training at Lackland Air Force Base in San Antonio, Texas. She graduated from basic training in July 1997 and went on to become an Air Force Security Police

Officer. Deanna is twenty-one and appears to be orchestrating her life in a very positive way. My temptation to interfere in her life is to quarterback her choices of boyfriends. I don't remember who said this, but a wise parent once wrote that he would just encourage his children since he had made plenty of mistakes in his own life. He figured his children would be able to determine what to do without his interference. Letting go is hard to do.

Deanna offers these reflections on her life as she now experiences it.

June 21, 1998

I am twenty-one years old, and I am serving in the United States Air Force. Now that I am no longer living with my parents, and I am not in the same role as a "preacher's kid," it is much easier to look back upon things that happened in my childhood. The most important thing I see is that my religious experience with my family as a child has given me structure and security. There are many times in my life when I have looked to God for answers and help. I have often wondered about the individuals who have no religious background and depend solely on themselves and society for enlightenment. It would be frustrating and seem hopeless to think you are going through life alone.

I also feel I have morals and values instilled in me through the influence of both my parents and their religious walk. This in turn has affected my decisions. Growing up in church has allowed me to look past peoples' imperfections and faults, and to find good in almost any situation I am faced with. The truth is that perfection is impossible, and no one is perfect all of the time.

When I was younger, I felt that our church life took over our family life to the point that we were not allowed to be human and to have our own faults and shortcomings as a family. I felt restricted as far as things I would choose to do or participate in because I was afraid of "what the congregation might think." You could always feel judgmental eyes watching you.

Overall, though, I would have to say my childhood as a "preacher's kid" was a beneficial and positive experience. I have been able to apply some standards and goals to my present life that have sustained me through some difficult times.

A REFLECTION ON PASTORAL MINISTRY FROM THE BACK PEW

I borrowed this closing heading from Episcopal clergyman, theologian, and friend, Archer Torrey, who wrote the following in a personal letter: "Satan is as active today as he ever was right in the front rows and the pulpits. If you want to find Jesus where two or three are gathered in his name, look in the very back row."[11] Therefore, I would guess that the back pew is a safe place to speak from. I pulled out some old diaries in which I penned the agonies of our "wilderness wanderings" between the summer of 1989 and the summer of 1990. In an entry for August 30, 1989, I recorded two pictures of Christ that Diana saw in a mental image. On the one hand she saw a confident, triumphant Christ, and on the other hand she saw an image of Christ, ". . . suffering on behalf of her—curled over—taking the pain and the humiliation Diana was experiencing."[12]

When I reflected on this entry, I thought of the overblown emphasis of the triumphant Christ in today's Christian theology and practice to the exclusion of the suffering Christ who continues to bear our sorrows and our losses. Life is a mix of triumph and tragedy. Life is not a Madison Avenue hype of carefree living where our only concern is which brand of toothbrush to use. I believe the mistake of the church today is to underplay the agony and imperfection of our human experience because it is not good business.

This brings me to a second concern that churches today are market-oriented rather than spirit-oriented in their reasons for existence. The stress for too many churches and denominations is to create a religion that will bring in the money. Comfortable theater seats, plenty of excess parking, media-perfect worship performances, and catering to the needs of middle-class and upper-middle-class families. All of this is done because it is good business. The money that flows in from the more affluent social classes in our society ensures the survival of religious organizations and also that the leaders will be amply paid. Church growth becomes not a mission to reach the lost but a business strategy to preserve the institution.

Since a prevalent motive for growing and expanding new and established churches is the money they will generate, the people who are closest to God's heart lose out again. These are not the triumphant, "we have got it together people." The people close to God's heart are the poor and hurting who huddle, as Archer Torrey says, in the back pews—if they are allowed in the church at all. In a market-driven worldview, where do you put the homeless person who would come to church poorly dressed and reeking with body odor? What about someone else from the wrong side of town who lacks the social graces of the affluent deep pockets? The ushers usher the unlovely out of too many cathedrals so the comfortable rich don't get upset. Nonetheless, the scriptures shout at us: "Do you not know that God loves the poor? You are kicking out the chosen people!"[13] Following are some excerpts from an article in *The Triplicate* (May 10, 1997). The article that was originally titled "Capstones" because capstones are the most important stones in the construction of a building (Acts 4:11).

> I don't think you can judge the success of a church by its attendance, the size of the sanctuary, or its material wealth. Further, the success of a churchcannot be measured by an abundance of programs or purity of doctrine. I believe the success of a church can only be measured by how that church treats people and who it is willing to serve.
>
> Consequently, I argue that the successful church creates an environment of love for human beings that does not cast aside persons whom the world has rejected. Such a church makes room for those "whose names weren't called when choosing sides for basketball," and for "those with ravaged faces," and for those with no power or influence. I dare say that the least of these are the chosen people that Jesus Christ seeks to rescue and give the highest honor.
>
> The Apostle Peter reminded the religious leaders of the Sanhedrin in Acts 4:11 that "He (Jesus Christ) is 'the stone you builders rejected which has become the capstone.'" In a similar way, I believe the poor, oppressed, and dispossessed will become our capstones in the emerging kingdom of God. We should therefore serve such persons well.[14]

A final observation before I leave this back pew concerns the fragileness of both life and being, which is inherent in all of us. One of my favorite plays is *The Glass Menagerie* by Tennessee Williams. The tragic heroine of that play, Laura Wingfield, is an extremely shy young woman who throughout the play is found playing with her collection of glass animals. According to Williams' description of the character, "A childhood illness has left her crippled, one leg slightly shorter than the other, and held in a brace . . . Stemming from this, Laura's separation increases till she is like a piece of her own glass collection, too exquisitely fragile to move from the shelf."[15]

In our own unique way, we all share the fragileness of Laura Wingfield. We could find our glass animals of security, health, reputation, and self-confidence shattered in moments of misfortune. Laura's leg was crippled. Jacob limped too after he wrestled with an angel (Genesis 32:24-32). We all have our defects. Some of us are better at hiding them than others. But makeup, brand-name clothes, and an expensive car are poor cover-ups for the basic need we all have of being loved by God and cared about by others. We walk with a limp and keep a very fragile menagerie of animals. Thus, the curled up Christ that Diana saw in her mental vision is as much needed by us as a gospel of triumph. Both of these images of Christ are in the Bible, and one cannot be excluded in favor of the other. We are strong and weak at the same time. Such are we who are this "pastor's family." Weakness and strength have been concurrent qualities of our lives together. We have depended utterly upon the grace of God. And as the maiden leans upon her beloved in the Song of Solomon (8:5), so too do we lean upon God as we continue our journey.

Epilogue

Psychiatrist Victor Frankl sought to understand the reason for his resiliency and his capacity to survive the death camp at Auschwitz during World War II. He concluded that a major reason for his survival was his purpose for living. Frankl's immediate purpose for living was to finish a book. The Nazis had confiscated a manuscript of his that was ready for publication, and Frankl attributes his capacity to survive the horrors of his imprisonment to his desire to rewrite this manuscript.[1]

When Frankl reflects on this experience, he concludes that meaning and purpose for living are not some grand and final meaning and purpose that extend far into the future. Instead, meaning and purpose are the potentials inherent in each single situation we encounter throughout our lives. Thus, the purpose that enabled Frankl to survive the Nazis was not a grand, final meaning; the meaning that sustained him was his proximate purpose to rewrite his manuscript.

Frankl doesn't deny that a grand, final meaning exists, but he asserts that meaning cannot be found until we experience the thousands of individual events that come before the finale:

> . . . consider a movie: it consists of thousands upon thousands of individual pictures, and each of them makes sense and carries a meaning, yet the meaning of the whole film cannot be seen before its last sequence is shown. However, we cannot understand the whole film without having first understood each of its components, each of the individual pictures. Isn't it the same with life? Doesn't the final meaning of life, too, depend on whether or not the potential meaning of each single situation has been actualized to the best of the respective individual's knowledge and belief?[2]

So my experience as a pastor—attempting on the one hand to be faithful to my calling, while on the other hand seeking to juggle time to fully love and care for my family—has been a journey of a thousand meaningful moments. Sometimes the events have appeared to be disconnected, and the moments of stress have been overwhelming.

Nevertheless, if Frankl is right, all of these thousand moments of meaning somehow connect, and, as in a movie, we will understand the end and the ultimate purpose because of what has taken place before.

The end has not approached: there is still much of this movie yet to be shown, and I guess, since it is my life, I am impatient to see the finale. Notwithstanding, I think some of the final purpose for my experiences and this book may be to illuminate what is wrong with the way the pastor's family has been treated in the history of the Christian community. If these wrongs are recognized and change occurs in Christian social consciousness, then my failures, my family's sufferings, and the years of struggle will be redeemed by this purpose.

On the other hand, I recognize that such a dream may never be realized, and the abuse of the pastor's family could persist. Where, then, could meaning be found in my otherwise seemingly purposeless entanglements? I suppose here is where my faith meets the greatest test.

As I draw the curtain on this story, and as I peer to dark corners of the stage looking for clues to the mystery of purpose in all we as a family have experienced, I know I have changed. I possess a sensitivity and tenderness for my wife and children that developed as we lived out our story. Further, I entered a deeper level of trust in Christ because I have been compelled to rely on him when questions are unanswered and my experiences have been difficult and strange. Consequently, these promises of Jesus Christ are my hope:

> I have much more to say to you, more than you can now bear. But when he, the Spirit of truth, comes, he will guide you into all truth. He will not speak on his own; he will speak only what he hears, and he will tell you what is yet to come. (John 16: 12-13, NIV)

I wait upon the future with hope.

Notes

Preface

1. Joan Berzoff, "From Separation to Connection: Shifts in Understanding Women's Development," *Affilia,* 4(1), Spring, 1989:45.

Chapter 1

1. Archibald Hart, "The Emotional Hazards of Ministry," A Doctor of Ministry Seminar, Pasadena, CA: Fuller Theological Seminary, May, 1988.

2. M. Scott Peck, *The Road Less Traveled* (New York: Simon and Schuster, 1978), 120-121.

3. James Street, *The Gauntlet* (Garden City, NY: Doubleday, Doran and Company, 1945), 173-174.

4. My use of "convicting" relates to a prevalent expectation among some parishioners that the minister will give sermons that will not only implicate "sinners" but also scare the wayward into living right. In Jonathan Edwards' sermon, "Sinners in the Hands of an Angry God," Edwards scared his congregation with images of a fiery judgment for the wrongdoer. Hence, even 300 plus years since Edwards lambasted his congregants, there are church members who still come to services to get a spiritual tongue lashing. This need for verbal punishment by the minister is acted out two ways.

First there are persons who feel guilty about bad habits or their lifestyle. Consequently, a convicting sermon helps people like this assuage their guilt. If a preacher chastises in his message, some individuals feel purged (at least for an hour) of the persistent habits that cause them so much guilt. I think such persons also look at a stern sermon as a way to bargain with God. A person may reason, "I am not willing to change my life, but I am willing to listen to the preacher tell me what I need to do. That must count for something." As an example, I remember some parishioners who asked me to tell them to quit drinking and smoking. I would not do that, and I put the responsibility for behavior back on the person who asked for my chastisement. This caused tremendous anger in some who were unwilling to take responsibility for their own lifestyle decisions.

Second, there are other parishioners who want the preacher to preach "convicting" sermons for "those other people" who cause trouble in the church and have such irritating mannerisms. This manipulation of the minister and his message has been called "pitchfork religion": In pitchfork religion, the minister's harsh message is pitched back to those who really need to hear it. An example of this behavior is found in a common after-church dialogue that goes something like this: "It is too bad Mr. or Mrs. So and So were not in church today. Our pastor preached a message that described perfectly the trouble they cause and the disgraceful lives they live."

These quirks of human nature continue to amaze me. Concurrently, "convicting sermons" (for the wrong reasons) rather than "convincing" is a most descriptive term for #6. The corrupted issues are more than just persuasion.

5. Melody Beattie, *Codependent No More* (San Francisco: Harper & Row, 1987), 31.

6. Jim Alsdurf and Phyllis E. Alsdurf, "The 'Generic Disease'," *Christianity Today,* December 9, 1988:30.

7. William Barclay, *The Daily Bible Study Series, The Gospel of Luke* (Philadelphia: The Westminster Press, 1975), 196.

8. Barclay, *The Daily Bible Study Series, The Gospel of Matthew,* 195-199.

9. Ibid.

10. Barclay, *The Gospel of Matthew,* 212.

11. Cameron Lee, *PK* (Grand Rapids, MI: Zondervan, 1992), 128-130.

12. For a detailed discussion on marriage vs. celibacy as expressed in 1 Corinthians 7, see Leon Morris, *1 Corinthians,* in *The Tyndale New Testament Commentaries,* R. V. G. Tasker (Ed.). (Grand Rapids, MI: Wm. B. Eerdmans, 1983), 105-123.

13. William Barclay presents a parallel discussion of celibacy as a choice for difficult service in the ministry. "How can that be? It can happen that a man has to choose between some call to which he is challenged and human love. It has been said, 'He travels the fastest who travels alone.' A man may feel that he can do the work of some terrible slum parish only by living in circumstances in which marriage and a home are impossible. He may feel that he must accept some missionary call to a place where he cannot in good conscience take a wife and beget children. . . . That will not be the way for the ordinary man, but the world would be a poorer place were it not for those who accept the challenge to travel alone for the sake of the work of Christ." (Barklay, *The Gospel of Matthew,* 207-208.)

14. Lee McGee, "Family," in *Dictionary of Feminist Theologies,* Letty M. Russell and J. Shannon Clarkson (Eds.). (Westminister John Knox Press, 1996.) A web site source—http:/www.yale.edu/adhoc/research_resources/dictionary/ (May 23, 1998).

Chapter 2

1. My school day usually began at 8:00 a.m. and ran until about 4:00 p.m. I drove a bakery truck from 9:00 p.m. until 3:00 a.m., six days a week. On the weekends I worked as an apartment manager, doing cleaning and running the office. The office time did provide opportunity to study.

Chapter 3

1. Jon Tevlin, "Why Women Are Mad as Hell," *Glamour,* March 1991:206.

2. Roy Oswald, Carolyn Taylor Gutierrez, and Liz Spellman Dean, *Married to the Minister,* (Ambler, PA: The Alban Institute, 1980), 109-133. (Part of the

resource material for the DMin Seminar, Emotional Hazards of Ministry, conducted by Dr. Arch Hart at Fuller Seminary, May 1988.

3. Cameron Lee and Jack O. Balswick, *Life in a Glass House* (Grand Rapids, MI: Zondervan, 1989), 148.

4. Edwin H. Friedman, *Generation to Generation* (New York: The Guilford Press, 1985), 23-24; Ray S. Anderson and Dennis B. Guernsey, *On Being Family: A Social Theology of the Family* (Grand Rapids, MI: William B. Eerdmans, 1985), 109.

5. Trevlin, "Why Women Are as Mad as Hell," 208.

6. Oswald, Gutierrez, and Dean, *Married to the Minister,* 115.

7. Wagner's observations were part of a discussion in a Church growth seminar conducted in the spring of 1989.

8. Lee and Balswick, *Life in a Glass House,* 29-30.

9. Oswald, Gutierrez, and Dean, *Married to the Minister,* 129.

10. Ibid.

11. John C. Howell, *Equality and Submission in Marriage* (Nashville: Broadman, 1979), 121.

12. Ibid., 93.

Chapter 4

1. Norman MacLean, *A River Runs Through It* (New York: Pocket Books, 1992), 1.

2. Ibid., 113.

3. Cameron Lee, *PK* (Grand Rapids, MI: Zondervan, 1992), 76-77.

4. Ibid., see the Preface.

5. Ibid., see Chapters 4 and 5, especially pages 75 and 93.

6. Ibid., 24.

7. Ibid., 131.

8. Ibid., 100-101.

9. Ibid., 82-83.

10. Part of a conversation with Anna Korling, a marriage and family counselor. This dialogue took place in 1994.

Chapter 5

1. Brad Darrach, "The War on Aging," *Life,* October 1992:36.

2. Ibid., 36.

3. William M. Pinson Jr., *The Biblical View of the Family* (Nashville: Convention Press, 1981), 55.

4. Ray S. Anderson and Dennis B. Guernsey, *On Being Family: A Social Theology of the Family* (Grand Rapids, MI: William B. Eerdmans, 1985), 32. Dr. Anderson contends that the biblical purpose for family formation is the relationship and responsibilities parents have to love, train, and socialize the child.

5. Ibid., 32.

6. Pinson, *Biblical View of the Family,* 57.

7. Mari R. Anderson and Judy Johnson, "Introduction to 1 Timothy," *Serendipity New Testament for Groups, NIV,* Third Edition (Littleton, CO: Serendipity House, 1990), 398,399.

8. Ibid., 398.

9. Ruth A. Tucker, *Private Lives of Pastors' Wives* (Grand Rapids, MI: Zondervan, 1988), 38-46.

10. Ibid., 38-46.

11. Ibid., 49-59.

12. Dr. G.W. Schweer referred to marital conflict in the John Wesley family during a course presentation on evangelism at Golden Gate Baptist Theological Seminary, Mill Valley, CA, 1981.

13. See Chapter 1 of *PK* to get a better picture of the struggle for identity PKs experience when attempting to live in a home and church setting that pressure PKs with competing expectations. Lee stresses in his opening chapter that PKs live in this environment with no choice to leave it. Adults, on the other hand, can choose to stay in or leave the environment. Concurrently, dissidence and insubordination are means PKs have of coping with untenable situations over which they have no control. Cameron Lee, *PK* (Grand Rapids, MI: Zondervan, 1992), 15-28.

Chapter 6

1. Dr. Archibald Hart in a presentation for a seminar: The Minister's Personal Growth and Skill Development, Doctor of Ministry Program (Pasadena, CA: Fuller Theological Seminary), April 26-May 6, 1988.

2. James 1:2-4 speaks of the blessing of trials. According to the passage, trials produce perseverance, and perseverance produces character qualities of maturity and completeness.

3. Peter Menconi, Richard Peace, and Lyman Coleman, *Family: Living Under the Same Leaky Roof* (Littleton, CO: Serendipity House, 1989), 37.

4. William Pinson, *The Biblical View of the Family* (Nashville: Convention Press, 1981), 98-99.

5. Herbert Fensterheim, PhD, and Jean Baer, *Don't Say Yes When You Want to Say No* (New York: Dell Publishing, 1975), 139.

6. Ibid., 133-134.

7. John Bradshaw, *The Family* (Deerfield Beach, FL: Health Communications, 1988), 52-53.

8. Ibid., 61-85.

9. Ibid., 49.

10. Ibid., 51.

11. I think maybe a hidden lesson in the story of the Prodigal Son was that the father gave unconditional freedom to his child when he gave him the inheritance. This, I believe, illustrates our spiritual relationship to Jesus Christ, which is based on the unconditional freedom of our will to make choices and live out the consequences of those choices be they good or bad.

12. Edwin H. Friedman, *Generation to Generation* (New York: Guilford Press, 1985), 27.

Chapter 7

1. Herbert G. May and Bruce Metzger, Eds., Commentary on 1 Samuel 4:1a, *The New Oxford Annotated Bible with the Apocrypha* (New York: Oxford University Press, 1977), 335.

2. Richard Peace, *Codependency* (Littleton, CO: Serendipity, 1991), 13, 14.

3. Melody Beattie, *Codependent No More* (San Francisco: Harper & Row, 1987), 29.

4. Ibid., 31.

5. Nancy Groom, *From Bondage to Bonding* (Colorado Springs, CO: Navpress, 1991), 21.

6. Peace, *Codependency,* 11.

7. Anne Wilson Schaef, *When Society Becomes an Addict* (San Francisco: Harper & Row, 1988), 30.

8. Schaef, quoting Wegscheider-Cruse. *When Society Becomes an Addict,* 29.

9. Ibid., 30. Note also Schaef's alternate spelling for *codependency.* The more accepted spelling does not hyphenate the term. However, Schaef does spell the word with a hyphen: *co-dependency.*

10. Groom, *From Bondage to Bonding,* 50-51.

11. Schaef, *When Society Becomes an Addict,* 29-30.

12. Herbert Fingarette discusses the difference between heavy drinkers and diagnosed alcoholics. He states there are heavy drinkers with broad problems related to the use of alcohol who deny their drinking is a problem. At the same time, these heavy drinkers would not be clinically diagnosed as alcoholics. Herbert Fingarette, *Heavy Drinking: The Myth of Alcoholism As a Disease* (Berkeley, University of California Press, 1989) 4-5.

13. I have no written documentation for the sculpture of the alcoholic family. The descriptions given come from intervention sessions I attended as a chaplain at Charter Hospital in Roseville, California, in 1990. The material was part of a presentation given by a physician doing research on the effects of alcoholism in the family.

14. Groom, *From Bondage to Bonding.* See Chapter 7, "The Freedom of Surrender."

15. Ibid., 156.

16. Ibid., 183.

17. Ibid., 200.

18. *Twelve Steps and Twelve Traditions* (New York: Alcoholics Anonymous-World Services, Inc., 1981), 41. This prayer has been attributed to Reinhold Niebuhr.

Chapter 8

1. Anne Wilson Schaef and Diane Fassel, *The Addictive Organization* (San Francisco: Harper & Row, 1990), 66.

2. Richard Peace cites the statistic given by Sharon Wegscheider-Cruse in Anne Wilson Schaef's book *Codependence Misunderstood and Mistreated* (San Francisco: Harper & Row, 1986), 14. Richard Peace, *Codependency* (Littleton, CO: Serendipity, 1991), 10.

3. This discussion was presented by Peter Wagner in a Doctor of Ministry seminar on church growth (Pasadena, Ca: Fuller Theological Seminary), March 6-16, 1989.

4. Robert H. Schuller, *Your Church Has a Fantastic Future* (Ventura, CA: Gospel Light, 1987), 281-282.

5. Robert E. Alberti and Michael L. Emmons, *Your Perfect Right* (San Luis Obispo, CA: Impact, 1986), 7.

6. Edwin H. Friedman, *Generation to Generation* (New York: The Guilford Press, 1985), 27.

7. Fred Jones, *Positive Classroom Discipline* (New York: McGraw-Hill, 1987), 84.

8. Ibid., 85.

9. Randolph Sanders and H. Newton Malony, *Speak Up! Christian Assertiveness* (Philadelphia: Westminster, 1985), 34, 35.

10. Ibid., 41.

11. Ibid., 41, 42.

12. Ibid., 25.

13. Ibid., 26.

14. Ibid.

15. Ibid., 229-230.

16. Friedman, *Generation to Generation,* 229.

17. Ibid., 229-230.

18. Peace, *Codependency,* 59. See the discussion—"On Being a Codependent."

19. Douglas Rumford, "How to Say No Graciously," *Leadership* (Fall, 1982), 96.

20. Friedman, *Generation to Generation,* 249.

Chapter 9

1. Diana, in her readings on PMS, had a reference at one time to Mary Todd Lincoln as likely being afflicted by PMS and/or menopause rather than being insane. According to the article my wife read, hormones may have played a major role in the behavior of Mary Todd Lincoln rather than just the supposed diagnosis of insanity which was given by medical authorities of her time. Nonetheless, the article that contained this information has since disappeared from Diana's collection of readings on PMS and menopause. Consequently, I contacted Roger Norton, who has a web site on the Internet that specializes in the life of both Mary Todd Lincoln and Abraham Lincoln. What follows is a small e-mail response to my inquiry on the possible influence of hormones upon the behavior of Mary Todd Lincoln:

Hello Dan. Your wife is indeed right on the money with what she told you. It has definitely been theorized that at least some of Mary's problems were menopausal in nature. Mary was 42 when she first arrived at the White House and just entering menopause. For example on page 55 of Victor Seacher's *The Farewell to Lincoln* it says, "When Mrs. Lincoln came to her high station she was going through menopause and the nervous system is often capricious. That must be borne in mind when judging her actions." Summing up a lot of books that I've read, other ailments which Mary suffered from include terrible migraine headaches, possible undiagnosed diabetes, arthritis of the spine, coughing spells, hallucinations, and even hyperthyroidism. Some folks have speculated that Mary was never insane—rather she suffered from Borderline Personality Disorder (if interested, see the web page at http://members.aol.com/BPDCentral/basicbpd.html for a discussion of this illness).

Although not directly related to your message, I came across the following paragraph on page 45 of *Abraham Lincoln: The Man Behind the Myths* by Stephen B. Oates:

> Still, their intimacy suffered in later years. After the birth of Tad in 1853, Mary contracted a serious gynecological disease which, in the judgement of one specialist, "probably ended sexual intercourse between the Lincolns." After that, both became increasingly active outside their home, Mary in trips and shopping expeditions and Lincoln in politics. In 1858, the year Lincoln challenged Stephen A. Douglas for his seat in the United States Senate, he and Mary had separate bedrooms installed when they enlarged and remodeled their Springfield home.

Who knows! Anyway, thank you for visiting my web site and for your positive comment. I appreciate it very much! Godspeed.

Sincerely,
Roger Norton

Norton, Roger. "Mary Todd Lincoln." RJNorton@worldnet.att.net (May 27, 1998).

Chapter 10

1. Gerald F. Hawthorne, Ralph P. Martin, and Daniel G. Reid, Eds., *Dictionary of Paul and His Letters* (Downers Grove, IL: InterVarsity Press, 1993), 225-229.

2. Burt Bacharach and Hal David, "Alfie," *The Anita Kerr Singers Reflect on the Hits of Burt Bacharach and Hal David,* Dot Records DLP-25906.

3. Eugene Peterson, "Spirituality and Ministry," A Doctor of Ministry Seminar, (Pasadena, Ca: Fuller Theological Seminary, October, 1988). The books cited from this seminar are as follows: Hans Urs von Balthasar, *Prayer* (San Francisco: Ignatius Press, 1986). Don Postema, *Space for God* (Grand Rapids, MI: CRC Publications, 1983).

4. The complete story of the two goats is found in Leviticus 16:1-22. The story of the ritual of the scapegoat is found in verses 20-22.

5. Bill Hybels, *Too Busy Not to Pray* (Downer's Grove, IL: InterVarsity Press, 1988), 11.

6. C. Peter Wagner, *Prayer Shield* (Venture, CA: Regal Books, 1992), 81, 90. Also, see all of Chapter 4.

7. Ibid., 102.

8. Ibid., 104-116.

9. Ibid., 116.

10. Ibid., 27.

11. Ibid. See all of Chapter 1, but especially pages 26-37.

12. Ibid., 31-34. Wagner gave the following New Testament passages as examples of Paul's five requests for intercession: 1 Thessalonians 5:25; Romans 15:30; 2 Corinthians 1:11; Philippians 1:19; and Philemon 22.

13. Ibid., 69.

14. Ibid., 70.

15. Ibid., 123.

16. Ibid., 125.

17. Ibid., 130.

18. Ibid., 158.

19. Eugene Peterson, *Working the Angles: A Trigonometry for Pastoral Work* (Grand Rapids, MI: William B. Eerdmans, 1987), 114. This comes from the opening of Chapter 8, which is titled, "Getting a Spiritual Director."

20. Ibid., 114-115.

21. Ibid., 115.

22. Ibid., 119.

23. Wagner, *Prayer Shield.* See Chapters 5 and 6 on receiving personal intercession.

24. Ibid., 158.

25. Peterson, *Working the Angles,* 119.

26. Ibid., 117-119.

27. I also have discovered some other potential weaknesses regarding authority as a result of taking an abbreviated Myers-Briggs assessment. I believe the test accurately assessed me as an ENFP (Extrovert-Intuitive-Feeling-Perceiving). One of the weaknesses an ENFP temperament triggers on a profile is, "Difficulty with structure and authority figures." This Kiersey Temperament Sorter (an abbreviated Myers-Briggs) was a class exercise for Social Work Practice (California State University, Sacramento: Redding MSW, EDP Program, September 17, 1994). The instructor was Ms. Beverly Short.

28. Wagner, *Prayer Shield,* 63.

29. Peterson, *Working the Angles,* 124.

30. Ibid., 125.

31. Ibid., 127.

32. Ibid., 121.

Chapter 11

1. Archibald D. Hart, "Minister's Personal Growth and Skill Development," A Doctor of Ministry Seminar (Pasadena, CA: Fuller Theological Seminary, April 25-May 6, 1988).

2. Eugene H. Peterson, "Spirituality and Ministry," A Doctor of Ministry Seminar (Pasadena, CA: Fuller Theological Seminary, October 17-28, 1988).

3. C. Peter Wagner, "Healing Ministry in the Local Church," A Doctor of Ministry Seminar (Pasadena, CA: Fuller Theological Seminary, June 5-9, 1989).

4. This is a paraphrase of Peter Wagner's "Axiom One" of church growth from C. Peter Wagner, "Church Growth I, The Four Axioms of Church Growth," A Doctor of Ministry Seminar (Pasadena, CA: Fuller Theological Seminary, March 6-16, 1989), 2.

5. Daniel Langford, "Grace in an Unexpected Place," *Decision,* February 1994, 32. Excerpts from this article were taken from *Decision* magazine, February 1994. ©1994. Billy Graham Evangelistic Association. Used by permission. All rights reserved.

6. Explanatory notes for John 1:1. *The New Oxford Annotated Bible with the Apocrypha.* Herbert G. May and Bruce M. Metzger, (Eds.). (New York: Oxford University Press, 1977), 1286.

7. Marshall Loeb, Managing Editor, "Editor's Desk: Ideas That You Can Profit By." *Fortune,* October 26, 1992, 4.

8. Roger von Oech, *A Whack on the Side of the Head* (New York: Warner Books, 1983), 14-16.

9. "Poor in Possessions, But not Poor in Faith," *The Planter: A Newspaper for American Baptist Church Planters and Friends,* 45 (Winter, 1998), 3. Used by permission of *The Church Planter* © National Ministries, American Baptist Churches, USA, Valley Forge, PA.

10. Edwin Friedman, *Generation to Generation* (New York: Guilford Press, 1985), 27-30.

11. Personal letter from Archer Torrey, Taebaek Kangwondo, Korea, November 29, 1997.

12. Author's untitled personal diary entry for August 30, 1989.

13. See especially James 2:1-7 and Luke 4:18-19.

14. Dan Langford, "From the Pulpit," *The Triplicate* (Crescent City, CA), May 10, 1997.

15. Tennessee Williams, *The Glass Menagerie* (New York: Signet, 1987), 21.

Epilogue

1. Victor E. Frankl, *Man's Search for Meaning* (New York: Washington Square Press, 1984), 126-127.

2. Ibid., 168.

Bibliography

Alberti, Robert E. and Michael L. Emmons. *Your Perfect Right*. San Luis Obispo, CA: Impact, 1986.

Alsdurf, Jim and Phyllis. "The Generic Disease." *Christianity Today*, December 9, 1981:30-38.

Alsdurf, Phyllis, and Alsdurf, Jim. "Getting Free: Addiction and Codependency in Christian Perspective." *Christianity Today*, December 9, 1988:29-46.

Anderson, Mari R. and Judy Johnson. "Introduction to 1 Timothy." *Serendipity New Testament for Groups, NI*, Third Edition, Ed. by Lyman Coleman. Littleton, CO: Serendipity House, 1990.

Anderson, Ray S. and Dennis B. Guernsey. *On Being Family: A Social Theology of the Family*. Grand Rapids, MI: William B. Eerdmans, 1985.

Arterburn, Stephen and Jack Felton. *Toxic Faith*. Nashville: Oliver Nelson, 1991.

Bacharach, Burt, and Hal David. "Alfie." *The Anita Kerr Singers Reflect on the Hits of Burt Bacharach and Hal David*. Dot Records DLP-25906.

Balswick, Jack O. and Judith K. Balswick. *The Family: A Christian Perspective*. Grand Rapids, MI: Baker, 1989.

Barclay, William. *The Daily Bible Study Series,* (Revised Edition) *The Gospel of Luke*. Philadelphia: Westminster Press, 1975.

Barna, George. *What Americans Believe*. Ventura, CA: Gospel Light, 1991.

Beattie, Melody. *Codependent No More*. New York: Harper & Row, 1987.

Beattie, Melody. *Beyond Codependency and Getting Better All the Time*. San Francisco: Harper & Row, 1989.

Bellah, Robert N. *The Good Society*. New York: Alfred A. Knopf, 1991.

Bellah, Robert N, Richard Madsen, William M. Sullivan, Ann Swidler, and Stephen M. Tipton. *Habits of the Heart*. New York: Harper Collins, 1989.

Berzoff, Joan. "From Separation to Connection: Shifts in Understanding Women's Development." *Affilia* 4(1) Spring 1989, 45.

Bradshaw, John. *The Family*. Deerfield Beach, FL: Health Communications, 1988.

Bradshaw, John. *Healing the Shame that Binds You*. Deerfield Beach, FL: Health Communications, 1988.

Bradshaw, John. *Homecoming: Reclaiming and Championing Your Inner Child*. New York: Bantam, 1990.

Branden, Nathaniel. *The Psychology of Self-Esteem*. New York: Bantam, 1987.

Brandt, David. *Don't Stop Now, You're Killing Me*. New York: Poseidon Press, 1986.

Cook, Jerry and Stanley C. Baldwin. *Love, Acceptance, and Forgiveness*. Ventura, CA: Gospel Light, 1983.

Curran, Delores. *Traits of a Healthy Family.* Minneapolis, MN: Winston Press, 1983.

Curran, Delores. *Stress and the Healthy Family.* San Francisco: Harper & Row, 1987.

Darrach, Brad. "The War on Aging." *Life,* 15(10), October 1992:33-43.

Egan, Gerard. *The Skilled Helper.* Monterey, CA: Brooks/Cole, 1986.

Fassel, Diane. *Working Ourselves to Death.* San Francisco: Harper & Row, 1990.

Fensterheim, Herbert and Jean Baer. *Don't Say Yes When You Want to Say No.* New York: Dell Publishing, 1975.

Frankl, Victor E. *Man's Search for Meaning.* New York: Washington Square Press, 1984.

Friedman, Edwin H. *Generation to Generation.* New York: Guilford Press, 1985.

Galli, Mark. Review of: *Clergy Families: Is Normal Life Possible?,* Paul Mickey and Ginny Ashmore. In *Christianity Today,* June 22, 1992:42-43.

Gangel, Kenneth O. and Elizabeth Gangel. *Building a Christian Family.* Chicago: Moody Press, 1987.

Groom, Nancy. *From Bondage to Bonding.* Colorado Springs, CO: Navpress, 1991.

Hart, Archibald. "The Emotional Hazards of Ministry." A Doctor of Ministry Seminar. Pasadena, CA: Fuller Theological Seminary, April 25-May 6, 1988.

Hart, Archibald. "Minister's Personal Growth and Skill Development." A Doctor of Ministry Seminar. Pasadena, CA: Fuller Theological Seminary, April 25-May 6, 1988.

Hawthorne, Gerald F., Ralph P. Martin and Daniel G. Reid, (Eds.). *Dictionary of Paul and His Letters.* Downers Grove, IL: InterVarsity Press, 1993.

Howell, John C. *Equality and Submission in Marriage.* Nashville: Broadman, 1979.

Howell, John C. *Christian Marriage: Growing in Oneness.* Nashville: Convention Press, 1983.

Hubbard, David Allan. "Why We Must Make Our Marriages Work." *Family Life Today,* September 1981:23-27.

Hulme, William E. *Managing Stress in Ministry.* San Francisco: Harper & Row, 1985.

Hybels, Bill. *Too Busy Not to Pray.* Downers Grove, IL: InterVarsity Press, 1988.

Ibsen, Henrik. *A Doll's House and Other Plays.* Translated by Peter Watts. New York: Viking/Penguin, 1965.

Ingram, Kristen. "Violence in Christian Marriages." *Virtue,* October 1985:30-31.

Jones, Fred. *Positive Classroom Discipline.* New York: McGraw-Hill, 1987.

Kelsey, Morton and Barbara Kelsey. *Sacrament of Sexuality.* Boston: Amity House, 1986.

Korling, Anna. Personal communication, 1994.

Kosnik, Anthony, Chairperson. *Human Sexuality.* A Study Commissioned by the Catholic Theological Society of America. Garden City, NY: Doubleday, 1979.

Langberg, Diane. "If Your Husband Doesn't Share Feelings." *Partnership,* May-June 1985:12-15.

Langford, Daniel. "Grace in an Unexpected Place." *Decision,* February 1994:32.

Langford, Daniel. "From the Pulpit." *The Triplicate,* Crescent City, CA, May 10, 1997.

Larson, Jim. *Growing a Healthy Family.* Minneapolis, MN: Augsburg, 1986.

Lee, Cameron. *PK.* Grand Rapids, MI: Zondervan, 1992.

Lee, Cameron and Jack Balswick. *Life in a Glass House.* Grand Rapids, MI: Zondervan, 1989.

Livingston, Diana, Director. *Crisis Line Worker/Advocate Training Manual,* Eureka, CA: Humboldt County Rape Crisis Team, 1992.

Loeb, Marshall. "Editors Desk: Ideas That You Can Profit By." *Fortune,* October 26, 1992:4.

MacLean, Norman. *A River Runs Through It.* New York: Pocket Books, 1992.

May, Herbert G. and Bruce Metzger (Eds.). *The New Oxford Annotated Bible with Apocrypha.* New York: Oxford University Press, 1977.

McGee, Lee. "Family." In *Dictionary of Feminist Theology.* Letty M. Russell and J. Shannon Clarkson (Eds.). Westminster John Knox Press, 1996. Web site source—http://www.yale.edu/adhoc/research_resources/dictionary/ (May 23, 1998).

Menconi, Peter, Richard Peace, and Lyman Coleman. *Family: Living Under the Same Leaky Roof.* Littleton, CO: Serendipity, 1989.

Morris, Leon. 1 Corinthians. *The Tyndale New Testament Commentaries.* R .V. G. Tasker (Ed.). Grand Rapids, MI: William B. Eerdmans, 1983.

Norton, Roger. "Mary Todd Lincoln." RJNorton@worldnet.att.net. Informational Web site.

Oates, Stephen B. *Abraham Lincoln: The Man Behind the Myths.* San Francisco: HarperCollins, 1994, 45.

Oden, Marilyn Brown. "Stress and Purpose: Clergy Spouses Today." *Christian Century,* April 20, 1988:402-05.

Oswald, Roy, Carolyn Taylor Gutierrez, and Liz Spellman Dean. *Married to the Minister.* Ambler, PA: The Alban Institute, 1980.

Peace Richard, Stephen Crowe, and William Cutler. *Codependency.* Serendipity Support Group Series, Lyman Coleman and Marty Scales (Executive Editors) Richard Peace (Support Series Editor), Littleton, CO: Serendipity, 1991.

Peck, M. Scott. *The Road Less Traveled.* New York: Simon and Schuster, 1978.

Peck, M. Scott. *A World Waiting to Be Born: Civility Rediscovered.* New York: Bantam, 1994.

Petersen, Eugene. *Working the Angles: A Trigonometry for Pastoral Work.* Grand Rapids, MI: William B. Eerdmans, 1987.

Petersen, Eugene. "Spirituality and Ministry." A Doctor of Ministry Seminar. Pasadena, CA: Fuller Theological Seminary, October 1988.

Pinson, William M., Jr. *The Biblical View of the Family.* Nashville: Convention Press, 1981.

"Poor in Possessions, But Not Poor in Faith," *The Planter: A Newspaper for American Baptist Church Planters and Friends,* 45 (Winter, 1998):3.

Postema, Don. *Space for God.* Grand Rapids, MI: CRC Publications, 1983.

Rumford, Douglas. "How to Say No Graciously." *Leadership,* Fall 1982:93-98.

Ryan, Dale and Juanita. *Recovery from Codependency.* Downers Grove, IL: Inter-Varsity Press, 1990.

Sanders, Randolph K. and H. Newton Malony. *Speak Up! Christian Assertiveness.* Philadelphia: Westminster, 1985.

Saul, D. Glenn and William M. Pinson Jr. *Building Sermons to Strengthen Families.* Nashville: Convention Press, 1983.

Schaef, Anne Wilson. *Co-Dependence Misunderstood—Mistreated.* San Francisco: Harper & Row, 1985.

Schaef, Anne Wilson. *When Society Becomes an Addict.* San Francisco: Harper & Row, 1988.

Schaef, Anne Wilson and Diane Fassel. *The Addictive Organization.* San Francisco: Harper & Row, 1990.

Schaeffer, Edith. *What Is a Family?* Old Tappan, NJ: Revell, 1977.

Schuller, Robert H. *Your Church Has a Fantastic Future.* Ventura, CA: Gospel Light, 1987.

Searcher, Victor. *The Farewell to Lincoln.* New York: Abingdon, 1965, 55.

Street, James. *The Gauntlet.* Garden City, NY: Doubleday, Doran, and Company, 1945.

Supporting Clergy Marriage: What Every PRC Needs to Know. Pastoral Relations Committee, American Baptist Churches of the West, Oakland, CA, July 1992.

Swartley, William M. *Slavery, Sabbath, War, and Women.* Scottdale, PA: Herald Press, 1983.

Tevlin, Jon. "Why Women Are Mad as Hell." *Glamour,* March 1991, 206.

Tolstoy, Leo. *Anna Karenina.* New York: Bantam, 1960.

Tolstoy, Leo. *War and Peace.* New York: New American Library, 1968.

Tucker, Ruth A. *Private Lives of Pastors' Wives.* Grand Rapids, MI: Zondervan, 1988.

Tucker, Ruth A. *Women in the Maze.* Downers Grove, IL: InterVarsity Press, 1992.

Twelve Steps and Twelve Traditions. New York: Alcoholics Anonymous-World Services, Inc., 1981.

Uhlenberg, Peter. "Reinforcing the Fragile Family." *Christianity Today,* January 16, 1987:31-33.

Urs Von Balthasar, Hans. *Prayer.* San Francisco: Ignatius Press, 1986.

von Oech, Roger. *A Whack on the side of the Head.* New York: Warner Books. 1983, 14-16.

Wagner, Peter. "Healing Ministry in the Local Church," A Doctor of Ministry Seminar, Pasadena, CA: Fuller Theological Seminary, June 5-9, 1988.

Wagner, Peter. "Church Growth I, the Four Axioms of Church Growth," A Doctor of Ministry Seminar, Pasadena, Ca: Fuller Theological Seminary, March 6-16, 1989:2.

Wagner, Peter. *Prayer Shield.* Ventura, CA: Regal Books, 1992.

Watson, Annette. "You Need to Minister to Your Spouse." *Pentecostal Minister,* Winter 1981:78-79.

West, Cornel. "Spinning Visions." *The Other Side,* July-August 1994:12-13.

Williams, Tennessee. *The Glass Menagerie.* New York: Signet, 1987, 21.

Index

Order Your Own Copy of
This Important Book for Your Personal Library!

THE PASTOR'S FAMILY
The Challenges of Family Life and Pastoral Responsibilities

_____ in hardbound at $29.95 (ISBN: 0-7890-0584-0)

_____ in softbound at $14.95 (ISBN: 0-7890-0585-9)

COST OF BOOKS_____

OUTSIDE USA/CANADA/
MEXICO: ADD 20%_____

POSTAGE & HANDLING_____
(US: $3.00 for first book & $1.25
for each additional book)
Outside US: $4.75 for first book
& $1.75 for each additional book)

SUBTOTAL_____

IN CANADA: ADD 7% GST_____

STATE TAX_____
(NY, OH & MN residents, please
add appropriate local sales tax)

FINAL TOTAL_____
(If paying in Canadian funds,
convert using the current
exchange rate. UNESCO
coupons welcome.)

☐ **BILL ME LATER:** ($5 service charge will be added)
(Bill-me option is good on US/Canada/Mexico orders only;
not good to jobbers, wholesalers, or subscription agencies.)

☐ Check here if billing address is different from
shipping address and attach purchase order and
billing address information.

Signature_____

☐ **PAYMENT ENCLOSED: $**_____

☐ **PLEASE CHARGE TO MY CREDIT CARD.**

☐ Visa ☐ MasterCard ☐ AmEx ☐ Discover

Account # _____

Exp. Date _____

Signature _____

Prices in US dollars and subject to change without notice.

NAME _____

INSTITUTION _____

ADDRESS _____

CITY _____

STATE/ZIP _____

COUNTRY _____ COUNTY (NY residents only) _____

TEL _____ FAX _____

E-MAIL_____
May we use your e-mail address for confirmations and other types of information? ☐ Yes   ☐ No

Order From Your Local Bookstore or Directly From
The Haworth Press, Inc.
10 Alice Street, Binghamton, New York 13904-1580 • USA
TELEPHONE: 1-800-HAWORTH (1-800-429-6784) / Outside US/Canada: (607) 722-5857
FAX: 1-800-895-0582 / Outside US/Canada: (607) 772-6362
E-mail: getinfo@haworthpressinc.com
PLEASE PHOTOCOPY THIS FORM FOR YOUR PERSONAL USE.

BOF96